DON'T LET EXECUTIVE FATIGUE ROB YOU OF SUCCESS... OR THE ENJOYMENT SUCCESS BRINGS

The fatigue that results from the daily stress of making crucial business decisions, creating new concepts, or sitting through lengthy meetings can be more debilitating than any physical labor. But by following the Hilton Head Executive Stamina Program, built around Dr. Miller's revolutionary concept of ACTIVE REST, you can help reverse the effects of executive fatigue... and improve the quality of your life, in the office and out.

Featuring:

- *The Resting-in-Motion routine.* A 20-minute regimen of light physical and mental exercises that will leave you feeling relaxed and refreshed.

- *The Power Snack.* A practical, low-calorie treat that provides an extra lift. For a change of pace, try the five Super Energy Drink Suggestions found in chapter 11.

- *The Best Choices List.* Guidelines for choosing dishes for maximum energy and minimum calories at restaurant meetings, banquets, and buffets.

- *The Lifetime Stamina Fitness Plan.* Helps you reach new heights of energy, endurance, and vitality with a combined routine of brisk walking and eight stamina-building exercises.

- *The Brain Booster.* A series of visualization techniques help you gear up for the day ahead, while the power of imagery allows you to take a quick "mental vacation."

PETER M. MILLER, Ph.D., is a clinical psychologist specializing in health, habit change, and motivation. Since graduating from the University of South Carolina, he has written over sixty scientific articles and five books, including the bestselling *Hilton Head Metabolism Diet.** In 1977, Dr. Miller founded the Hilton Head Executive Health Institute®, an internationally known health retreat that has attracted top executives from around the world.

*Also published by Warner Books.

The Hilton Head EXECUTIVE STAMINA PROGRAM

Peter M. Miller, Ph.D.

WARNER BOOKS

A Warner Communications Company

WARNER BOOKS EDITION

This Warner Books Edition is published by arrangement with
Rawson Associates, 115 Fifth Avenue, New York, N.Y. 10003

Warner Books, Inc.
666 Fifth Avenue
New York, N.Y. 10103

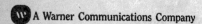 A Warner Communications Company

Printed in the United States of America

First Warner Books Printing: July, 1988

10 9 8 7 6 5 4 3 2 1

To my father,
Purdy Miller,
who taught me more about vitality,
stamina and success in life
than he will ever know.

Contents

Acknowledgments

▼

I am greatly indebted to the staff and consultants of the Hilton Head Health Institute for helping me formulate and develop the elements of *The Hilton Head Executive Stamina Program*. I want to thank Bob Wright who has been both invaluable in maintaining the high caliber of our nutrition program and so generous with his time and knowledge. I also want to thank Roger Sargent, Ph.D., for his support and critical evaluation of the program and for keeping us attuned to developments in the fields of health and nutrition.

I want to acknowledge the valuable editorial assistance and support of Eleanor Rawson and Toni Sciarra of Rawson Associates.

I especially want to thank my wife, Gabrielle, who has been and will continue to be my requisite partner in life. She is truly an unsung hero, without whose assistance, hard work, courage, support and love, the Hilton Head Health Institute would still be just a dream.

I owe a great deal to my son, Michael, and my daughter, Melanie, for their support and encouragement; they make their father's life richer simply by being who they are.

Finally, I am grateful to Stanley and Victoria for their constant companionship during my long hours of writing.

"Let me tell you the secret that has led me to my goal. My strength lies solely in my tenacity."

LOUIS PASTEUR

"The heights by great men reached and kept
Were not attained by sudden flight,
But they, while their companions slept,
Were toiling upward in the night."

HENRY WADSWORTH LONGFELLOW

1
▼
The Secret
Every Executive
Needs to Know

Everyone in the business world today knows how demanding and competitive corporate life can be. Executives are always searching for that certain something, that "edge" over the challenges they must face every day. They realize that effort, motivation and hard work are not enough to guarantee success in the top corporations. In the fast-paced world of business, everybody who wants to excel is willing to drive himself or herself to the limit just as much as the next person. Everyone wants that key job or that crucial contract just as badly as you do.

Despite this high level of competition, many executives successfully make it to the top. And they do it with as many or maybe even more hardships than the next person. To top it off, they often make it look easy!

What is the secret behind these executives who edge out the competition and perform at peak capacity? What do corporate leaders such as Lee Iacocca of Chrysler, David Kearns of Xerox, T. Boone Pickens of Mesa Petroleum,

Robert Goizueta of Coca-Cola, John Welch Jr. of General Electric, John Akers of IBM, and Alfred Brittain III of Bankers Trust in New York, have that others don't? After all, the combined pay (including bonus and stock gains) of these seven chief executives in 1984 was in excess of $38 million! They must be doing something right.

My Search for the Secret of Executive Stamina

Several years ago I set out to find the answer to this question. I was already familiar with the popular books on business excellence and motivation. These books either tell you what makes companies (as opposed to people) successful or they psych you up with inspirational "you-can-do-it-too" messages on employee motivation and teamwork. These publications can be very useful in company operations and planning, and helpful, at least temporarily, in charging you up to "get in there and give it all you've got." Unfortunately, the long-term benefits they provide are poor because they don't give you the skills necessary to keep you going strong on a day-in and day-out basis.

My ultimate answer to what makes top executives so successful came from two sources: first, my role as founder and director of the Hilton Head Health Institute where I have had a first-hand opportunity to observe and study executives from large and small companies, and second, my years of research as a clinical psychologist.

Located on Hilton Head Island, South Carolina, the Institute enjoys an international reputation as one of the top health, fitness and stress-management centers in the world. Ten years ago this health institute was just a dream of mine. As a clinical psychologist specializing in health, habit change and motivation, I had spent the first 15 years of my career testing methods of motivation and life-style change in a university medical center. I had published over 60 research articles and written two books aimed primarily at a professional audience. My dream was to put my research into practice, to see how it worked in the "real world." And what better a real world than that of the busy corporate executive who faces enormous challenges every day?

I decided to establish a corporate retreat where an executive could go to maximize both personal and professional potential by developing a healthier, more fulfilling life style. This dream has been a reality for the past 10 years. The Hilton Head Health Institute has become a world-famous executive health retreat, where business managers from around the globe come to participate in 12-day intensive training sessions during which they learn the secrets of corporate fitness, health and stamina. Since they are away from their normal business routines, they also have an opportunity to "learn by doing." I put them on a daily routine that enables them to practice what I am preaching. They experience the physical and mental benefits of our program firsthand.

During their stay they practice the *Hilton Head stamina nutrition and fitness plan* on a daily basis. I teach them what to eat and when to eat for maximum stamina. They practice my simple physical fitness plan, which is designed to build up energy reserves in the body. Once learned and reinforced, the techniques are easily adapted to day-by-day corporate life.

During the past 10 years, thousands of men and women from IBM, Polaroid, Rockwell International, Marietta Aerospace, American International Underwriters, and many other companies have begun new, more vital and more successful corporate lives through my organization's work with them. In fact, the Hilton Head Executive Stamina Program grew out of my research with these executives.

In addition to my own research, I have carefully evaluated the most revealing scientific studies on work performance and business success that have been conducted over the past 50 years. These corroborated my own findings and enabled me to develop a program that is on the cutting edge of what we know about human energy.

The Secret of Executive Success Revealed

My own research results were based on lengthy interviews with executives who were coming to the Hilton Head Health Institute to develop better levels of fitness. My sample included men and women ranging in age from 30 to 70 and in career positions from middle management to chief executive officer. All enjoyed a certain level of success and all were upwardly striving, achievement-oriented corporate executives. After a much more detailed analysis, however, I found that some stood out from the rest in terms of the *consistency* of their success.

These world-class executives were able to beat out the competition time and time again. Their tenacity and consistency set them apart from other high-level achievers.

At first I thought that these top executives were perhaps more clever, intelligent, creative and aggressive or better organized than their peers. Such was not the case. These qualities varied from person to person; none was the key ingredient.

Actually, their secret is quite simple. The most successful executives maintain an endurance level that enables them to create and sustain a surge of high-powered energy even after grueling hours of work and travel. They have learned how to turn the negative stress of an intense, hectic schedule into *positive energy* and *vitality.*

By sustaining peak energy, they consistently outshine their mentally fatigued colleagues. They not only look and feel energized but they also convey an appearance of strength and vigor that gives them a *psychological edge* as well.

They simply outlast the competition physically and emotionally and are able to accomplish more than their competitors in less time.

When questioned about their stamina, these people seem perplexed and simply say they are doing what comes naturally. They are not aware of any special formula for maintaining peak energy. A closer look reveals that they are, indeed, doing several essential things that contribute to their strengths. I will share these with you in the chapters that follow.

Through studying such corporate stars at the Institute, in the management seminars I conduct around the country and through research in general, I have developed a program that teaches these skills. More important, I have had the opportunity to test the system with a wide range of executives over several years at the Institute and elsewhere.

With the help of the step-by-step program that I will describe to you, those who have learned this system and incorporated it into their lives on a daily basis find that they can:

- Increase mental and physical stamina on even the most hectic days.
- Turn business stress into positive energy in a matter of moments.
- Sharpen powers of concentration no matter what the hour.
- Improve memory.
- Revitalize during tiring negotiating sessions.
- Avoid jet lag on long flights.
- Accomplish more in less time.
- Experience a real sense of being in control of every aspect of life—at work and away from it.

The Case of Donna and Fred

To give you an example of the kind of people who seek assistance and the changes that occur in their lives as a result of the program, let me tell you about Donna and Fred, an overstressed working couple. Donna ran her own management consulting business while Fred was the assistant director of marketing for a well-known soft drink company. Both were in their late 30s and both were very ambitious. Their schedules were full of meetings and travel; working late even on weekends had become a way of life. Neither wanted to work so many hours forever, but they were willing to pay the high price for success at least for a few years in order to achieve their career goals and enjoy the fruits of their labors at a later date. Besides, both liked the challenges of the business world and felt stimulated by their busy lives.

I first met Donna and Fred at a workshop on stress management. I was on a panel of speakers discussing ways in which business managers could learn to handle stress more effectively. After the talk, Donna and Fred came up to find out more about my ideas on developing and sustaining the kind of energy that would make them more efficient in every aspect of their lives. They were smart enough to know that their enormous workloads could burn them out before they accomplished their goals in the business world. In fact, attending the stress management workshop was really their first step in taking better care of themselves. They were a very close couple, supportive of each other's careers—and they wanted to keep things this way.

They had seen the relationships of too many working couples destroyed because the couples couldn't sustain enough energy to keep an intense career *and* a close, personal relationship going at the same time. They had simply run out of emotional and physical energy by the end of the day.

Donna and Fred were determined to put maximum intensity into career *and* marriage and were searching for a program to give them the stamina that such intensity requires. I'm happy to say they found it in our program.

When I started them out on the stamina plan, we found a major deficit in their lives was physical activity. Both had jobs that required them to be extremely busy but highly sedentary. And they were so tired when they weren't working that they spent most of their spare time sitting, talking to one another, watching television, reading or casually entertaining close friends at home. While these activities relaxed them, they had no exercise benefits.

I taught Donna and Fred the elements of the program that emphasize stamina through a fitness routine. Their eating habits, although sometimes erratic, were already quite good, so we didn't have to change much there. When I first mentioned exercise, however, they were put off.

"Fred and I just don't have time," Donna said. "Besides we barely have enough energy as it is. Exercise would just take more energy away from us."

I can assure you, just as I did Donna, that my stamina exercise plan takes *minimal time* and will not interfere with the precious little free time you already have. In addition, exercise and physical fitness will give you a tremendous energy boost. Do not confuse the weary feeling you have at the end of a long business day with *bodily* fatigue. You might feel completely worn out, but you are suffering from mental overload and muscular fatigue due to *inactivity*. What you really need is physical activity—not just any physical activity—but the kind that adds stamina: the kind I will be outlining for you.

Once Donna and Fred began the program, they amazed themselves with the results. Now they follow my fitness plan religiously. They were pleasantly surprised that it did not involve joining a health club or becoming enslaved to a rigorous exercise routine.

Fred put it this way:

"Donna and I enjoy your stamina fitness plan. We needed something that would fit into our busy lives, even when we're traveling, and you gave it to us. We're both feeling more vim and vigor than we've felt in a long time. I'm not nearly as tired at the end of the day and I have much more endurance in my work. Donna has even had a couple of clients comment on her new-found energy. They wanted to know what pep pill she was taking!

"Both of us feel more relaxed, too. Your program has helped us work out job stresses, especially those that we can't do anything about. We enjoy each other more in our spare time and we're looking for more recreational activities that require physical activity. In fact, we've already found a great one—our sex life has returned!"

Reaching Your Maximum Potential

I don't want you to use my system simply to work 16 hours a day. You can achieve maximum stamina only by making sure you have an adequate balance of work and play in your life. It's easy to burn out if you're not careful. Work is *one* element of your life and *one* element only. I realize that on some days it may seem to be the only aspect of your life that you have time for, but this should not be the norm.

This is exactly why I designed the Hilton Head Executive Stamina Program in the first place. I want you to be able to do *more* work in *less* time and to be more efficient and more creative in that work so that you can do it well *without* letting it consume your life.

You should treat yourself *at least* as well as you do your business. What if your health and stamina were the business? What if you were to evaluate your healthy life-style habits as you evaluate your business performance? Well, it's sad to say, but based on past performance, you might have gone bankrupt a long time ago!

It's time to change all that. If you are in charge of your business life you can also be in charge of your body. Perhaps the problem is that you haven't been as consistent in controlling your body as you have in controlling your business. You can change that imbalance without taking anything away from your success at work, however. This system is so easy for you to put into practice that it will become a natural part of your life style in no time!

I want you to be able to use some of the extra energy time I'm giving you for your personal life as well. You must be able to work with intensity, play with intensity and love with intensity.

I am talking about psychological as well as physical fulfillment. You must make a conscious decision to improve the quality of your life and health; otherwise, living can become a dull, energy-draining routine of schedules and responsibilities. When this happens, you have weeks when you feel as though you are just putting in your time. You do your work and stay busy, but somehow something is missing; you go through the motions but without joy, without challenge.

Under these conditions it's probably a given that there is not enough balance to your life. Let me explain what I mean by relating the case of one executive whom we saw at the Institute.

The Case of the Overworked Advertising Executive

Andrew is a 51-year-old senior administrator for a large advertising firm. He is married, with a grown daughter who lives away from home. Andrew's wife, Lillian, is a successful part-time teacher and author of children's books.

Two years ago, Andrew came to the Institute for help with hypertension, elevated cholesterol and chronic fatigue problem. He was totally dedicated to his job, working 12 to 14 hours each weekday and bringing work home on weekends. His wife, although far from satisfied with the little time they spent together, led a busy life with her writing and teaching. Andrew worried that his work patterns were threatening his health, marriage and social life but was afraid of losing momentum in his career if he devoted less time to his work.

Soon after I started Andrew on our executive nutrition and exercise program I also took aim at rebalancing his lifestyle. I first asked him to imagine his life as a set of balloons of different sizes. Each balloon would represent a different aspect of his life, and the relative size of each balloon would correspond to the amount of time and energy invested in each life area. I then used the following illustration to summarize the balance (or, rather, the lack of it!) in his life.

Since there is a limit to any person's time and energy each day, the balloons are depicted as a "closed" air system; that is, they share a common air supply that has a *fixed* limit. This means that a change in the air supply of any one balloon will correspondingly affect the air in one or more of the other balloons. If Andrew wanted to spend more time and energy with his wife, the air for his "wife" balloon would have to come from one of the other balloons. This would necessitate less time and energy for work, self, friends, etc.

As you can see, Andrew's "work" balloon far outshadows his other balloons. His "self" balloon, which consists of what he does for himself for his own benefit, is very small in comparison to any of the other balloons.

Women executives often have a more complex set of balloons, since they frequently must maintain a large "work" balloon and an equally large "family" balloon. The result is

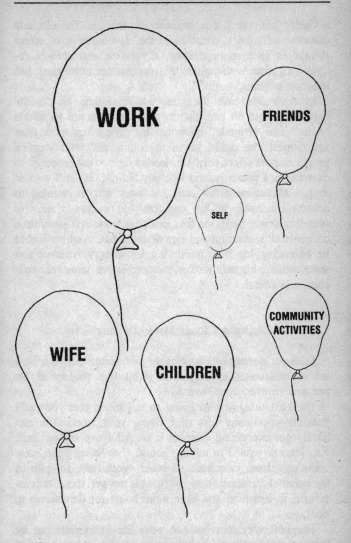

Figure 1-1 Andrew's Lifestyle Balance

a "self" balloon that is microscopic in size. The ultimate outcome of such a situation is the development of stress symptoms such as headaches, depression and chronic fatigue, together with unhealthy, inconsistent nutritional and exercise patterns.

In Andrew's case the goal was to inflate his "self" balloon quite a bit and also to add slightly more air to his "wife" and "friends" balloons. By giving him more time for himself, he could begin to follow my total stamina program more effectively. He needed time to eat properly, to exercise as I prescribe and to enjoy his life. He still wanted to put maximum effort into his work but he wanted to accomplish more in his business life in less time. By spending fewer hours on less essential work and more time on his health, stamina and emotional needs, Andrew would be balancing his life, improving his energy reserves and transforming himself into a more effective manager, husband and friend.

Taking a Closer Look at Your Life

Take out a sheet of blank paper and sketch out your own set of balloons. Do they look a bit like Andrew's? Or perhaps are they even worse?

The first thing you're going to tell me is that you can't possibly spend any less time doing your work. You can hardly get everything done as it is. All I can say is: Trust me. I know what I'm talking about; I've heard these same comments from thousands of other executives. In spite of their initial protests, they were able to get more accomplished in less time and have more hours for themselves to boot.

The best way to rebalance your life is to start out by looking at your "self" balloon and considering how you can add to it. If you begin by trying to eliminate work activities you'll never get anywhere. You'll come up with too many reasons why it's impossible.

"Self" activities are those that bring you pleasure and satisfaction. They do not have to accomplish anything other than personal fulfillment. I realize that you are also fulfilled by your work and your family life, but these "self" activities are a little different from that. They are more "you" oriented. I don't necessarily mean self-centered, because some of these activities could very well include others that you care about. I want you well-rounded, not selfish.

Remember, "self" activities must not be harmful to your health or be self-destructive. This eliminates the excessive intake of sweets, for example, even though eating sweets might give you a great deal of pleasure.

You might begin by looking for "self" activities that:

- You haven't done in a very long time (perhaps since you were quite young)
- You always wanted to do but never did
- You don't do often enough.

Get out a sheet of paper and list every possible activity in these categories that you can think of. Don't be cautious. Don't put something down and then change your mind because it would be silly for someone like you to do such a thing.

Here's the list that Andrew compiled:

Play handball more often.
Read more science fiction.
Travel to the Orient.
Try woodworking.
Learn to fly an airplane.
Take golf lessons.
Buy an English bulldog.
Buy an old house in the country and fix it up.

Become an actor.
Get deeper into photography as a hobby.
Go whitewater rafting.
Entertain friends more often.
Take a course in watercolor painting.
Take my wife and daughter to Hawaii for two weeks.
Go on an archeological expedition.
Write a novel.
Live in a small village in Italy for a month.
Learn to play the piano.
Buy a Maserati.
Learn to speak fluent Italian.
Attend more sporting events.
Take long-distance bicycle trips with my wife.

To start inflating your "self" balloon, try one of the activities on your list each month. What you want to do is sample your list to see which activities you might like as recreational pursuits. Give each one a chance. Don't give up on any activity just because you're not good at it. If you are an achievement-oriented person, this may be difficult at first.

For these "self" activities, you don't have to be proficient; you should be doing these for fun—not to be the best. This is especially important for you to remember if you are a hard-driving, competitive person in business. You need a more relaxing recreational pursuit for balance. So if you paint landscapes that look like garbage dumps, it really doesn't matter. You must strive to enjoy the *process* rather than the product.

If some of the activities on your list are more involved, requiring a major life change or a major financial or time commitment, take them in stages. In Andrew's case, he wanted to buy an older house in the country and renovate it gradually on weekends. He started out simply by taking trips to the countryside on weekends and looking over the classified ads for country property. He was then free to pursue this possibility in increments. In fact, after a while he found that he enjoyed these outings with his wife more than the prospect of actually purchasing a house.

Andrew's desire to become an actor was partially fulfilled through a local community theater group. Although he played only small parts and mostly helped to build sets, he enjoyed himself immensely. He also met a wide circle of new friends.

Of course, you'll never have the time or the inclination to do everything on your list. That's really not the point. The idea is to *explore* new personal horizons, to set new personal goals and to see that it *can* be done. By doing this you'll become a more vital, energetic person in both your work and your personal life.

What the Hilton Head Executive Stamina Program Can Do for You

I want to get you started on these stamina attitudes and life changes right away. These changes are a lot easier to make than you think, if you follow my program and take them one step at a time. My program will make you feel so energetic, right from the beginning, that you'll feel like a new person ready for a more vigorous, vital life.

Keep in mind that the Hilton Head Executive Stamina Program is a *proven system that can increase your business efficiency, concentration and stamina by as much as 50%*. It will not radically alter your day by requiring you to eat strange foods, to take dozens of vitamins or food supplements or to exercise for hours at a time.

The Hilton Head executive stamina program is based on sound, scientific principles. It has paid off for thousands of executives from all over the world and now it can pay off for you, too. Through this book, the results of my own and my colleagues' work are available to every executive, not just the few who are able to enroll in the Institute itself.

Now that you know what the program is and what it can do for you, take the quiz in Chapter 2. It is the first step toward understanding your stamina level and the specific ways you can benefit from this book.

Remember, the program is as much a philosophy of life as it is a health and stamina program. Get ready to take charge of your life and to feel more energetic than you ever thought possible!

2
▼
The Stamina Quiz

Before I go into detail on the nature of business endurance and how to improve it, let's stop and evaluate just how much you might need this system. If you wonder how much more stamina *you* need, just take a sheet of paper and write "yes" or "no" to each of the following questions. If you are somewhere in the middle on a question, try to decide whether it is more often "yes" than "no" or *vice versa*.

1. I feel there are not enough hours in the day to fulfill my obligations to my work and family.
2. I experience a downward shift in energy and concentration late in the afternoon.
3. I tire easily when I am under work or personal stress.
4. Short breaks or time away from work have, at best, only a temporarily revitalizing effect.
5. I eat erratically during the business week.
6. I probably drink more coffee than I need.

7. I probably drink more alcohol than I need.

8. I frequently bring work home from the office.

9. My powers of concentration and attention at work are not as high as they could be.

10. Long business trips leave me drained and fatigued.

11. I have difficulty finding enough time in the day to exercise as regularly as I should.

12. Sometimes I feel tired even when I wake up in the morning.

Give yourself 10 points for each "yes" answer and rate yourself on the scale below.

Total Score	Stamina Category
0 to 10	Above average
20 to 40	Average
50 to 80	Below average
90 to 120	Poor

If you scored 50 or above, you definitely need this program. With a score between 20 and 40 you have about an average amount of stamina. You should see marked improvements by following the guidelines in this book.

Improving Your Score

I don't want you to become discouraged by your score. Probably 90% of busy, hard-driving executives would discover they do not have as much stamina as they should. And you probably don't need a test to tell you that you could do with more energy—you've probably been telling yourself the same thing lately. If you're overworked and putting a great deal of yourself into your work, I'll bet you are a great procrastinator when it comes to *you*.

A client of mine, Ed, had the same problem. Ed is the chief financial officer for an international pharmaceutical firm. He came to me several years ago in preparation for a series of meetings regarding the takeover of several small drug companies. The negotiations were delicate and, to further complicate matters, each of the five companies involved was located in a different country.

For the next six months, Ed and his staff were going to be traveling thousands of miles, trying to stay at their peak levels of efficiency as they did so. To add stress, the CEO wanted little or no publicity about these meetings until the last possible moment.

Ed came to the Institute and participated in the 12-day executive stamina program. Ed had been feeling a little sluggish lately; he just wasn't at his mental or physical peak and he knew it. He had been meaning to do something about it but just couldn't find the time to get off the corporate merry-go-round for a while. Besides, he really didn't know how to go about finding more energy and stamina.

Ed put it this way, "It's not that I'm so fatigued that I can't do my job. It's just that I know that I can put more into it. On an energy scale from 1 to 10, I'm at 5. No one else even realizes it except perhaps for my wife and kids. I'm not as mentally sharp as I can be and I'm certain it's affecting my concentration and judgment. And I must be ready for these negotiations."

The trouble with Ed is that he waited until an important series of meetings was coming up before he tried to do anything about his problem. Many times in each of our lives, it take a mini crisis to precipitate action about a problem. It's like an out-of-shape athlete wanting me to turn him into an instant champion a month prior to the Olympic Games.

Don't get me wrong. You can improve your stamina in the business world in just a few days, but if you want maximum stamina and energy that last over time, you must put this lifetime stamina regimen into practice week after week. The point is that you don't have to wait until your company is planning a week-long think tank to improve your stamina. The time to begin is NOW. I am offering you a proven, practical program, so there's no need to put it off any longer.

Ed is a perfect example of the success that can be achieved by following the program. As might be expected from his comments, Ed scored a 100 on the Stamina Test. This put him in the "poor" stamina category. During his stay at the Institute, I put Ed on our super stamina nutrition plan, consisting of four high-energy meals per day (in Ed's case, they were low calorie meals). During the 12-day program Ed lost 10 pounds and came down to a fighting weight of 180 pounds (just about right for his 6'1" frame). He also started my physical fitness program designed for maximum energy and stamina in a minimum amount of time. In addition, Ed learned the secrets of our resting-in-motion program and the techniques needed to supplement and reinforce the basic stamina regimen. All of the details of this physical and mental endurance program will be shown as we proceed.

After just a few days Ed was invigorated and ready for the challenges of his upcoming trip. In fact, his comment to one of my staff was, "I never thought I could feel this energetic. My mind is just full of new ideas. I haven't been able to think this clearly in years."

Ed was ecstatic with his results. In addition to the fitness and nutrition regimen, he responded particularly well to our brain booster routine, designed to infuse energy and power into his memory and creativity. Repetition was the key, with Ed listening to the brain-booster audiotapes over and over again.

Several weeks after he left the Institute, I received a

telephone call from Ed in England. The following excerpt from his conversation tells the whole story:

"Well, I'm about half way through my travels and I'm feeling great. We just wrapped up the third deal last night and I was really on top of things. At 2 a.m., mine was the only brain in full gear, and I came up with an unexpected solution to a stumbling block that clinched the deal two days earlier than scheduled.

"The thing that's really amazed me is that I've been able to continue your stamina program even during all my travels. I know you told me it wouldn't be that difficult or time consuming but I was skeptical. Now I'm a firm believer in your program and especially in the results."

Since Ed's experience I have heard from hundreds of others just like him who have had similar results. Men and women from every type of business and profession imaginable have become charged up with new reserves of energy, not just for a day or two, but on a permanent basis. I want to make you one of that group.

3

▼

The Six Factors That Cause Executive Fatigue

Exactly what is meant by the words *energy* and *stamina*? Webster's dictionary defines energy as "vitality of expression," "power exerted forcefully" and the "capacity for doing work." Stamina is defined as "staying power" and is derived from the Latin word *stamen*, meaning "thread of life spun by the Fates" (the three goddesses of classical mythology who determine the course of human life). My program can be your "thread of life" in the business world.

As I define it, high-energy stamina is *the ability to display peak mental and physical vitality for an extended period of time without yielding to fatigue*.

While we all experience peak energy from time to time, these peaks are generally brief and difficult to maintain. Many factors in corporate life are at work to rob you of energy and stamina. Executive fatigue is very different from the physical fatigue that results from strenuous manual labor, athletic performance or even lack of sleep.

22

Executive fatigue is much more debilitating than these other forms of fatigue because it has both physical and psychological components. The body and mind wear down after hours of sitting in meetings, writing voluminous reports, paying close attention to conversations, making spur-of-the-moment decisions, remembering essential details of a business arrangement, creating new ideas and concepts and rushing to meet deadlines.

The fatigue, loss of concentration, memory lapses and feelings of being ''all drained out'' are chiefly the result of six factors ranging from tired muscles to lack of oxygen. Let us examine what I call the *Six Executive Fatigue Factors*.

Factor 1: Muscle Fatigue

The mental exertion involved in executive work takes more physical effort than most people realize. Muscles in the face, forehead, neck, shoulders and upper back tense up as a result of maintaining certain body positions. Sitting for prolonged periods at a desk or staying on top of things at lengthy business meetings are major culprits. Normal daily business dealings cause you to expend energy constantly, but at a less than maximum level. This continual idling of your ''engine'' causes muscle tension that in turn, results in physical fatigue. Muscles involved in mental work become even more tense in times of family or work stress. As biofeedback studies have shown, stress causes increased muscle activity in the shoulders, neck and forehead. Muscle fibers are being activated even though you are not moving— of course, you are not even aware that this is happening.

Nervous habits compound the problem. Which of the following nervous habits contribute to your muscle fatigue? In a notebook, write down whether you find yourself doing any of the following:

1. Clenching your jaws
2. Grinding your teeth in your sleep
3. Fidgeting with pen, desk accessories, etc.
4. Clenching your fist
5. Nodding frequently during conversations
6. Using many gestures when you talk
7. Uncontrollably twitching facial muscles
8. Tensing muscles when angry
9. Tapping desk or tabletop with fingers
10. Pursing lips/mouth when tense

This involuntary tightening of muscles when they are at rest is known as *static tension*. Static tension results in biochemical changes in muscles, leading to a buildup of a metabolic waste product known as *lactic acid*. This is the same byproduct that builds up in the body during strenuous exercise and accounts for muscle soreness and pain. In your life as an executive, the accumulation of lactic acid is not as extreme; therefore, your sensation will be one of overall weariness as opposed to specific muscle soreness or cramping. Fatigue increases in direct proportion to the amount of lactic acid in your bloodstream.

Muscle fatigue also inhibits the production of a substance in your body called *acetylcholine*. This substance assists the transmission of nerve impulses. When muscle fatigue suppresses acetylcholine production, smooth mental and physical functioning is disrupted. Thinking is not as sharp and response time slows down.

Passive forms of rest such as catnaps and meditation fail to eliminate these basic physiological reasons for fatigue. The Hilton Head Executive Stamina Program provides a regimen of moderate muscular activity designed to counteract the buildup of lactic acid. In fact, you will learn routines that *actually will drive* the fatigue-inducing agent *out of your muscles*. This cleaning of the muscles can be accomplished with little effort so that you feel complete refreshment in just a few minutes.

Factor 2: Nutrient Fatigue

Prolonged muscular fatigue and mental concentration cause a reduction in muscle glycogen. This is called *nutrient fatigue*.

Glucose or *blood sugar* is a naturally occurring sugar found in food. Extra supplies of glucose that are stored in muscles or in the liver are called *glycogen*. Blood glucose and glycogen serve many purposes in your body, but their major role is that of an energy source. In fact, *glucose is the major source of energy for your brain* and is absolutely necessary for the proper functioning of nerve tissue. Brain cells are almost completely dependent on glucose for mental alertness and stamina.

Glucose comes from carbohydrates. Simple carbohydrates are sweets such as candy, cake, pastries and pies. While these foods provide energy, they are not the best source of glucose for your body. Sweets can raise your blood sugar level too quickly, often resulting in a drop in energy two to three hours later. I'm sure you've experienced the late afternoon "blahs," but perhaps never attributed this slump to what you had for lunch that day. Sweets are usually "empty calories" as well, providing few essential nutrients and usually adding unnecessary weight. Carrying around extra pounds can certainly add to the burden of your day and drain your energy even further.

I once proved this point to a client in a dramatic way. Sarah, the publicity director for a large publishing house in New York, consulted me recently because she was overweight, overworked and completely lacking in stamina. As a result of my program she lost 25 pounds, started my exercise plan, reorganized her life and renewed her energy level. After about six weeks of her new, stamina lifestyle I asked her to try a little test. Using a weighted belt and ankle weights, we put her former 25 pounds back on her body. She agreed to wear the weight for 2 days to see how the 25 pounds affected her. She was astonished by her drop in energy:

"No wonder I felt so tired all the time. Twenty-five extra pounds really makes a difference. I'm going to remember this feeling every time I eat!"

The best sources of glucose are the *complex carbohydrates*. These include fruits, vegetables, bread, cereal, potatoes and pasta. Glucose derived from these foods is generally absorbed more slowly than that from sweets and is more likely to provide you with *long-term energy* without the characteristic ups and downs of simple carbohydrate intake.

Estimated Amount of Caffeine
(a Real Energy Robber)
in Popular Products

Coffee (1 cup)	125 mg
Instant Coffee (1 cup)	100 mg
Decaffeinated Coffee (1 cup)	4 mg
Tea (1 cup)	75 mg
Cola Drinks (12 oz)	35 mg
Cocoa (1 cup)	8 mg
Bittersweet Chocolate Bar (1 oz)	20 mg
Aspirin (1 tablet)	32 mg
Pills to Keep You Awake (1)	100 mg

The Hilton Head executive stamina nutritional plan provides a more than adequate energy base for your day-to-day business life. In addition, our *power snack* gives you an instant energy boost on those longer, more tedious work days or on busy meeting days when you can't always eat right.

If you happen to be on any of the high-protein or low-carbohydrate diets for weight reduction, you are particularly prone to nutrient fatigue. Your muscles and brain simply do not have the glycogen reserves necessary for the long haul. The low-calorie version of our Hilton Head executive stamina nutritional plan is a much better choice to burn calories, stimulate metabolism and keep your energy system going strong.

One of the most revolutionary and startling findings in recent months is that *too large an intake of certain vitamins can cause fatigue, apathy and lack of endurance*. If you are taking too much vitamin E, B$_6$ or D you may be doing yourself more harm than good. The irony is that you probably are taking these vitamins to *increase* stamina while, in fact, they may be doing just the opposite. This is such an important and controversial area as far as stamina is concerned that I am devoting an entire chapter to vitamin supplements. Refer to Chapter 9 for specific information on why certain *energy* vitamins may be robbing you of the stamina you need.

Factor 3: Dehydration Fatigue

You probably don't realize that the gradual loss of body fluids during the day is a major contributor to fatigue. *Loss of body water results in lethargy and muscular discomfort.* Nor do you have to be sweating profusely or urinating frequently to lose valuable body fluids. *The process of water loss occurs during the day without your realizing it.*

People who work in stuffy, dry offices lose a great deal of water by evaporation through the skin and through the lungs. If you travel a lot on business, you should be aware that the rapid circulation of dry air in an airplane can result in your losing as much as *two pounds* of water in a 3½ hour flight! Fluid loss is even more rapid if you drink coffee, tea, caffeinated colas or alcohol. All of these serve as diuretics, taking even more water out of your system.

About three years ago, Bob, a 45-year-old sales executive, was following the Hilton Head Executive Stamina Program but was still experiencing increasing fatigue as the day wore on. As I analyzed his habits, I noticed that he was drinking about five cups of coffee during his morning schedule, two glasses of wine with lunch and more coffee in the afternoon. Bob rarely drank liquids other than these. His energy reserves were literally being drained out of him. When I discussed my observations with him he was skeptical.

"How could the coffee and alcohol I drink have that much effect on me?" he asked.

I advised him to switch to decaffeinated coffee, eliminate the wine with lunch and drink several glasses of carbonated water throughout the day. After the third day of this routine, Bob called me to report the results.

"I'm totally amazed," he exclaimed. "My energy level shot up on the first day. I didn't realize how lackadaisical I was feeling. That caffeine really had a negative impact on me. I feel like I've discovered a magic energy potion," he said.

"You have, Bob," I agreed, "it's called H_2O!"

Note: If you drink a lot of caffeinated coffee and decide to switch to the decaffeinated kind, you may experience a few days of sluggishness and headaches due to caffeine withdrawal. These difficulties are usually temporary.

The Hilton Head Executive Stamina Program fights dehydration fatigue in two ways. First, it increases your intake of carbonated, decaffeinated fluids. *Carbonated* beverages enter your bloodstream faster and revive you more quickly than uncarbonated ones. This is due to the fact that the gas in the bubbles creates pressure that forces the liquid quickly through the walls of the capillaries in the lining of your stomach and small intestine. Also, the carbonation stimulates the small valve, known as the *pyloric sphincter,* which functions as a door leading from your stomach to your *duodenum* (the upper section of the small intestine). By stimulating the valve to open, the carbonated liquid is forced rapidly into the small intestine where it can more readily head directly into the bloodstream. (Now you know why you get tipsy on champagne faster than on the non-bubbly varieties of wine.)

The second way this program counteracts dehydration fatigue is through high-energy snacks that also are high in potassium. Potassium and sodium are salts that regulate fluid balance in your body. Potassium, however, is a better choice to regulate fluids since sodium, which is in regular table salt, has some health risks. Many people should limit their sodium intake to no more than 2000 mg (one teaspoonful) a day. The health concern with sodium is that high salt intake has been significantly correlated with elevations in blood pressure. Potassium has not been shown to elevate blood pressure.

In my program, I recommend a daily late-afternoon snack, consisting of one portion of potassium-rich fruit. Portion sizes vary with each fruit and I will provide equivalent substitution charts so you will know exactly how much of the potassium-rich foods such as oranges, melons, bananas and tomatoes to eat each day. Details of exactly when and what to eat for maximum effect from the Power Snack will be outlined in a later chapter.

Note: While certain high blood pressure medications reduce body water, these diuretics should *never* be discontinued as a means of increasing energy. My program will work for you whether you are on these medications or not.

Factor 4: Oxygen Starvation Fatigue

Another important component of executive fatigue can be an insufficient supply of oxygen to the brain. Sustained mental effort during long periods of physical inactivity causes erratic breathing patterns: You begin to take uneven or shallow breaths, which reduces the oxygen in your system needed for mental clarity. Memory, attention span and overall alertness suffer. What's even worse, you may not even realize that your alertness is waning. At least when you recognize a drop in mental energy you can summon up more caution in your business dealings.

My executive stamina program includes special deep-breathing exercises designed to increase the supply of oxygen to your brain and to counteract mental fatigue. Simple rest and relaxation have a counterproductive effect since they slow breathing and heart rate and further reduce needed oxygen.

Factor 5: Stress Fatigue

Many years ago, Dr. Hans Selye first described how devastating stress could be to the mind and body. One of the most stressful environments that exists certainly is the world of the corporate executive.

Selye noted that there is a relatively specific response of the body to different "stressors": If you are very cold, your body will shiver to produce heat; if you run quickly to save a child from an oncoming car, your heart beats faster to strengthen your muscles with oxygenated blood.

Selye also observed, however, that all stressful circumstances—physical or psychological—put an overall strain on the body above and beyond these specific responses. The body is required to adapt to the changes in its system. This more *nonspecific response to demands placed on the body* he labeled *stress*. The nonspecific nature of stress takes its toll on the body's energy reserves in subtle but nonetheless devastating ways.

To illustrate this point, let's examine how your body deals with stressful events during what is called the *general adaptation syndrome*. This syndrome consists of three stages. During stage 1, the *alarm phase*, your brain recognizes the stressful circumstance and through the action of hormones stimulates heart rate and blood pressure. Your body is now ready for what is known as "fight or flight." In times of *life threatening* stress, such as a physical attack, the alarm phase prepares you either to challenge your attacker or run away to safety. Unfortunately, your body responds in exactly the same way to *psychological* stress even though real "fight or flight" is inappropriate. Your stress response is the same whether the stressful event happens to be an unreasonable boss or an attack by a ferocious lion.

The second stage of stress, the *resistance phase*, involves your body's attempt to cope and adapt to the stressor. You try your best to calm down, reason with yourself, talk out your frustrations with your spouse or seek other ways to find relief.

If you are exposed to enough stressful circumstances day after day and you have difficulty keeping up with them, you enter into the *exhaustion phase*. During this phase, fatigue sets in and your body begins to break down. Stress symptoms occur: You find it difficult to sleep; you suffer from headaches; you drink too much; you eat too much; and you yell at the kids. Your body simply begins to wear down, to burn out. Since stress is a response to *any* demand, stress-causing events can be either positive or negative. Any change, whether it is a promotion or a demotion, triggers the stress response and drains your energy.

The Seven Major Causes of Executive Stress

- Time interruptions
- Lack of ultimate decision-making power
- Unclear performance criteria
- Slacking-off of subordinates
- Inadequate feedback from top management
- Office politics
- Too much work, too little time

Here is a list of stress symptoms that would most certainly affect your stamina. In a notebook, check off those that apply to you.

Signs of Stress Fatigue

- Inability to concentrate
- Feelings of weakness
- Emotional tension
- Insomnia
- Headaches
- Decreased appetite
- Increased appetite
- Nightmares
- Reduced sex drive
- Early morning awakening
- Irritability
- Depression
- Periodic rapid heart pounding
- Moodiness

Depending on your personality, it may not be the number of stressors in your life that cause problems, but rather how you *perceive* them. Some successful business leaders (known as type-A personalities) are more prone to both stress and heart disease. Stress-prone personalities are highly competitive, always in a hurry, forceful in speech, hard-driving, time-oriented and very precise about details. They talk, walk and eat rapidly. They are impatient and quick-tempered.

If you are a type-A executive, you are capable of taking a relatively neutral situation and turning it into a stressful one. For example, have you ever become extremely upset and angry over being caught in a traffic jam or being delayed five minutes for a meeting by someone else's tardiness? Of course, anyone might become mildly annoyed by these circumstances. The type-A personality might brood over these episodes and let them set the tone for a bad day.

Rest and relaxation have only a partial influence on these people. *In fact, type-A executives actually become anxious when they try to relax.* They are more affected by action than inaction. This is why my executive stamina program is so successful with this type of person.

My *resting-in-motion routine* disrupts the "fight or flight" stress response and serves to drain off stress-induced fatigue.

Factor 6: Motivational Fatigue

Without proper motivation and incentive you can quickly become bored and fatigued. Even when motivation is high, long hours of business cause a drift in attention. Momentary lapses in your goals and purpose can allow the other person to take advantage and come out on top.

An important part of mental fatigue is related to a drift in your focus of attention. During important business meetings you must be singleminded: You must have a single purpose and concentrate your total energies on the goal at hand and the incentives that will carry you through.

Since the central nervous system and the muscular system of the body are constantly active, motivating yourself is not so much a problem of arousing yourself to action *as it is of patterning and directing your actions*. I'm sure you have had days when you had a great deal to do, more than you could possibly accomplish. As the day wore on, you probably felt stressed and fatigued by the workload. You certainly were busy, running from one task to the next. When you took stock at the end of the day, you may have realized that even though you were terribly busy, you actually accomplished little. Your motivational arousal was there, but the patterning and direction of your behavior were being hampered by fatigue and stress. The resulting effect was that you flitted from one activity or problem to the next, too jittery to settle and focus on only what you could handle in the time allotted.

In addition, constant repetition of the same nerve cell sequences in the brain caused by repetitive mental work leads to boredom and fatigue. Brain cells can tire out from monotony and fail to respond properly. As we'll see in the next chapter, *rather than needing rest*, the brain actually needs the mental and physical stimulation provided by the executive stamina program *to rejuvenate itself*.

This was exactly the problem with June, an executive client of ours who works in a middle management position for a major textile manufacturer. June had worked her way up the ladder from salesperson to district sales manager in just five years. The challenges of the corporate world excite June and she looks forward to future promotions. A dedicated employee, she takes her responsibilities seriously.

In her position as district sales manager, she supervises eight area managers who, in turn, have six to eight salespeople responsible to them. When she was first promoted to the district level she accepted the challenge head-on and was really charged up about her new position. After about six months, however, fatigue and listlessness set in. These were new experiences for June, since work has always stimulated her. She became quite upset over her lethargy and mental dullness. She expressed her problem to me in this way:

> "I don't know what's happening to me. I'm just so tired all the time. I feel like falling asleep every afternoon, even though I get plenty of sleep at night. What's wrong with me? What am I doing wrong?"

Since June had not had a medical examination in over three years, the first thing we did at the Institute was to have our physicians give her a thorough workup. They determined that June was in excellent health and nothing in the tests indicated any medical reason for her fatigue.

Next, we evaluated her on my six fatigue factors and found that she was suffering most from a combination of stress fatigue and motivational fatigue. June was so caught up in her work that she failed to take into account the stress she had placed on her body. Within the last six months she had been promoted, moved from the outskirts of a moderate-size southern city to downtown Chicago and taken on a great deal more responsibility. In addition, many of the area managers now working for her resented the fact that, although she had not been with the company as long as they, she had been promoted to the district level before any of them. June felt that as a woman and as someone with less experience in the business, she had to prove herself to be a better manager than any of her predecessors. Because of this, her new job became her life.

On top of all this, June's new job actually turned out to be a lot more boring and repetitive than she ever imagined. When she was lower on the totem pole she dealt directly with customers or other salespeople who met with customers on a daily basis. She was a people person and enjoyed the close interaction with others. In contrast, her new position involved a lot of traveling to keep track of the area managers and hours of going over sales reports and writing her own sales reports to the home office.

After a few months in her new job, fatigue set in and the quality of her work deteriorated.

> "I feel mentally and physically exhausted," she said. "I don't find any challenge in this job. I spend hours going over monotonous reports on sales figures. All this was new and challenging at first, but now it's just a dull routine. I find myself daydreaming about doing more exciting work."

At first she considered quitting and finding a more challenging position with another company. Then she concluded that resigning was not the answer. She liked the company. They had been good to her and if she stuck to her present position and did a good job she surely would be promoted again. Quitting was the easy way out; it was giving up and she was not going to do that. Besides, that was exactly what many of the area managers wanted her to do. She decided that the only way she was leaving was in an upward direction.

Now that she had made a decision to stay put, what was June to do about her fatigue? She consulted me at this point. A friend of hers had overcome a similar problem at my Institute a few months before and had recommended that June consult me about a solution to her dilemma.

June put 100% effort into the Hilton Head Executive Stamina Program. I got her started immediately with our stamina nutrition and fitness plan. Our quick-energy *resting-in-motion* routines that include both physical and mental exercises to stimulate the body and brain helped her enormously in overcoming the boredom that was inherent to her work. Through our regimen, June was able to expand her horizons and receive more stimulation from people and activities outside of her work setting.

In the final analysis, June developed the stamina and energy she needed to be an effective manager in only a few weeks. With her new energy reserves she felt more satisfied with her job and was completing her work in about half the time it used to take her. The psychological stamina she developed really helped her cope with her area managers who, despite their earlier resentments, began to show a real respect for her abilities.

After she had been following the program for about a month, one of the managers commented, "I don't know what's happened to you but I've never seen anyone with the energy and drive you have. You never seem to run out of steam. And you seem to have enough left in you to have an enjoyable life away from work."

Little did he know that just four short weeks before, June had so little energy that she could hardly make it through the day. Now, even the long hours of travel didn't bother her. Our basic rules for business travel had turned business trips from drudgery into just another day at the office.

I'm happy to report that a year after June first contacted us she was named "Manager of the Year" by her company and "Business Woman of the Year" by a local community group. I'm sure another promotion is just around the corner. In fact, June has set her sights on becoming the president of her company, and I believe she's going to make it.

June is only one of many who have profited from the Hilton Head executive stamina program. Executives have different fatigue factors that affect them and our program is designed to counteract all of them. In fact, it wouldn't be unusual if you suffered from every one of them.

Now it's time to get into more detail. I'm going to show

you how this program is different from anything you have tried before and exactly how it can begin building your stamina today.

Note: Chronic fatigue and lack of stamina—particularly in combination with other symptoms—can signal a wide variety of medical disorders (e.g., heart trouble, anemia) and psychological conditions (depression) requiring professional treatment. If you have not had a recent medical examination you should consult a physician about your fatigue symptoms before starting this or any other self-help program.

4

▼

Resting-in-Motion: Why It Energizes You as Nothing Else Can

It may surprise you to know that catnaps, relaxation, extra sleep and meditation *do not* revitalize executives on busy schedules. While resting can reduce tension and produce relaxing mental and physical effects, it actually can reduce the efficiency of your work performance. Resting reduces heart rate, metabolism, circulation and muscle tone. San Diego State University scientists found that *rest breaks have a detrimental effect on attention span and reaction time*.

Imagine a marathon runner sitting down for a 10-minute rest and relaxation break halfway through the race. He might be relaxed, but not *refreshed*. In fact, he would have lost his state of peak arousal during which his mental and physical skills are most acute.

The same is true of you as a manager. For years I taught corporate executives relaxation and meditation techniques as part of my stress management seminars. My goal was to reduce stress levels and make tension more manageable. I always was frustrated by the fact that few of my clients used these techniques when they needed them. While some would practice on a regular basis, they did so on weekends or after arriving home from work in the evening. During busy, tense business days they rarely relaxed.

When questioned, they gave me a variety of explanations. One vice president from Xerox said:

> "Whenever I try to relax during a long negotiating session it really doesn't help. It brings me down and makes me sleepy. I can't seem to concentrate as well. So I just don't do it."

An engineer at Marietta Aerospace observed:

> "I often have one crisis after another to deal with during the day. I tried taking a 15-minute relaxation break in the mid-morning and mid-afternoon. It had a very negative effect on me. You see, I thrive on stress. I need to keep up a certain level of stress; it helps me think and stay on top of things. These meditation periods relaxed me, but I felt I had lost my sharpness."

A financial manager from IBM said:

> "I travel all over the world, running from one of our offices to another. The travel really drains me, especially when I have to be mentally prepared for an important presentation an hour after I arrive in another country. My facts must be straight and I must be able to think quickly on my feet. Your relaxation technique can be very helpful at the end of the work day, but when I try to use it during the day or before a meeting, it just makes me more anxious. Actually, I try to psych myself up rather

than calm down. I need tension to keep me at my best.''

What many executives fail to understand is that in addition to psyching themselves up, they also need methods of providing the body with rest. Psyching yourself up over and over again during a relatively short period of time robs your body of energy needed for more psyching. After a while, you find you are drained and unable to reach your peak level of arousal.

I'm sure you have watched competitive weight lifters prepare to lift a formidable load. They often glare at the bar, take several deep breaths, yell, scream or do whatever it takes to become aroused, then lift the weight. Obviously, they do not compete every day. But, as an executive, you must lift your weight load several times a day, week after week. Burnout becomes a real possibility without adequate rest. But what kind of rest does an executive need?

Which Rest Is the Best Rest?

Obviously, passive rest and relaxation have detrimental effects on performance. In addition, rest alone will not attack the basic physiological and psychological reasons for loss of stamina. None of the six executive fatigue factors will respond to rest breaks because passive rest cannot:

- Rejuvenate glucose needed for energy.
- Restore fluid levels.
- Reduce lactic acid in muscles.
- Reestablish proper brain cell activity.

But stimulation—of the right kind—can accomplish all of these things!
The best rest of all, the one that can relax and stimulate

you at the same time, is what I call *resting-in-motion*. This concept is at the heart of the Hilton Head Executive Stamina Program.

Resting-in-motion refers to a 20-minute regimen of light physical and mental exercises that rest the body and rekindle energy reserves like no other method. I have taken this idea to its maximum limits, and expanded it into a total physical, nutritional and mental regimen that will ensure you high-energy stamina under any business condition.

As early as 1965, Belgian researchers tested a similar idea with workers in a large manufacturing company. Employees were randomly assigned to one of two different types of "rest" periods. One group sat and rested during a 10-minute break. The other group performed a routine of mild calisthenic exercises during their break. Following the 10-minute break the researchers found striking differences in the quality of work between the groups. The employees who had been physically active were far superior to the others on all measures of memory, decision-making abilities, eye–hand coordination, fine motor control and mental acuity.

More recently, studies in numerous medical and psychological journals have indicated that physically active rest breaks for executives lead to enhanced mental concentration and a significant decrease in feelings of physical and mental fatigue. My own studies have not only corroborated these results but also have shown enhanced creativity, memory and decision-making abilities after active rest breaks.

What's Wrong with the Good Ole Coffee Break

Probably the worst kind of rest period during your business day is the traditional coffee break. The coffee break really does nothing to revive you: the caffeine in the coffee or soft drink you consume will further deplete your energy reserves by robbing you of even more body water. The physical inactivity characteristic of coffee breaks does nothing to recharge your mental energy. Moreover, if you continue to do business during your coffee break it is not really a rest at all.

Is a Different Kind of Work Break All You Need?

While a more physically active rest break during your work day, such as the one I'll be teaching you, is tremendously helpful, it may not be enough to reenergize you fully. Remember, stamina is lost in several ways related not only to a sedentary desk job, but also to nutritional influences, fluid balance, stress, motivation and even oxygen supply to your brain. Certainly, if you are a 40-year-old executive who is 30 pounds overweight, smokes a pack or more of cigarettes a day, drinks 3 or 4 glasses of wine every evening and gets no exercise, you're going to need a lifetime stamina regimen that goes beyond a simple quick pick-me-up routine.

Don't be alarmed. I can just hear you now. You're saying, "No! This is one of those programs where I have to completely change my life, become an exercise fanatic and deprive myself of practically everything." You're probably also thinking that in a busy schedule like yours you simply don't have the time to spend on some kind of new program.

Let me put your mind at ease. Believe me, I know the kind of hectic life you lead. I have been working with people like you for years. Through others like you, I have listened to your problems and concerns every day. Based on years of professional experience and study, I have developed a program that is ideally suited for you, the corporate executive. It is tailored to the kind of life style you have chosen to lead in the business world.

This program definitely does not take a great deal of time. I am going to make your life easier, not more difficult.

The executive stamina program is a simple, step-by-step system that can be applied with ease to your business life. It is a *total stamina plan*. It does *not* take a lot of time to put into practice. And you will *not* feel deprived.

Remember, this program is designed to provide you with a basic lifetime energy plan of nutrition and fitness. In addition, once you have the basic system in operation, you will learn booster techniques to overcome the Six Executive Fatigue Factors and tap into super stamina on days that are particularly hectic. These *resting-in-motion* routines can take as little as 20 minutes out of your business day. Don't you think new heights of ENERGY, ENDURANCE and VITALITY are worth 20 minutes of your time?

Basically, the Hilton Head executive stamina program is divided into five elements:

1. The super stamina nutrition plan
2. The stamina fitness plan
3. The 20-minute resting-in-motion routine
4. The 3 minute mini-refresher
5. The stamina attitude/stress management plan

In the following chapters, I will describe each element, giving you a simple formula for putting each phase into practice. I want this program to change your life just as it has done for others. I want to give you the stamina you deserve—the stamina that is long overdue in your life.

5

▼

Fuel for the Executive Engine: Ground Rules for Stamina Eating

I told you earlier that my *resting-in-motion* routine could bring you increased energy in as little as 20 minutes per day. Well, it can! But, let's face it, if you are carrying 35 extra pounds of body fat, rarely exercise, eat a lot of fat, sugar and high calorie foods, and drink alcohol, coffee or colas every day, my system of increased stamina will be of limited help. That's just common sense.

I'm sure you realize that achieving total stamina and energy takes a new commitment to your health and life. I stress the word *new* as opposed to *total*. I certainly understand that you have many commitments in your life. Still, I don't want to kid you into thinking you can simply do a few quick pick-me-up routines each day and get all the stamina you need in spite of the fact that you are abusing your body in just about every way possible.

I will promise you this, though. If you are willing to change just a little, the program will give you more energy and better feelings about yourself than you ever have had before. If you are willing to eat a little better and be just a bit more active, then my *resting-in-motion*, stamina-enhancing routine will bring you more energy and success than you've ever dreamed of.

Believe me, I've seen it happen. I can help you but you must be willing to help yourself. I will show you the way and make it as easy as I can for you. You just can't expect to stay physically unfit and accomplish everything your colleagues are accomplishing. You might succeed for a while, but it won't last.

Eating Right: Easier Said Than Done

Eating sensibly in the business world is easier said than done. I'm sure you have a very good idea of what kinds of food are good and bad for you. With business lunches, traveling and eating on the run, however, you probably feel lucky just to get anything at all to eat. Even when the correct choices are available you might not have the energy, self-discipline or presence of mind to make the best nutritional choices. After all, if your stamina is low, you must channel the little energy you have toward the business at hand. During the business day, your body simply takes second place to everything else around you.

This is exactly why you may have had trouble following other healthy dietary plans. Mine is *the only complete nutritional plan that takes your life as an executive into account*. For example, how can you follow rigidly set meal plans if you don't even know whether you'll be eating tonight's dinner with business associates, at home with your family, at the airport waiting for your flight to Dallas (the trip you found out about only an hour ago) or alone in a hotel room?

The Hilton Head executive stamina nutritional plan is so simple to follow that you won't even realize you're doing anything differently. It really doesn't take any more time for planning and preparation than what you are already doing.

In devising my nutritional plan, I made certain assumptions about your life as a business manager:

1. You probably eat many of your meals in restaurants.

2. Your scheduled eating times often are erratic (dinner may be any time between 7 p.m. and 10:30 p.m.—or nonexistent—just a sandwich on the run, if you are lucky.

3. While you want to eat right, you have neither the time nor the inclination to figure out details regarding specific calorie counts or the exact nutritional composition of each food you put in your mouth.

4. Your schedule for meetings, meals and just about everything fluctuates with the tide of the business day and you must develop a flexible routine.

My system takes each of these assumptions into account to provide you with a plan that is practical, easy to follow and, most important, effective. You won't have to become an amateur nutritionist or keep extensive records on your eating patterns. You won't have to follow a rigid food plan made up of foods that are difficult to find. You won't even have to give up most of your favorite foods.

Your Policy Manual for Stamina Eating

The food that you eat every day is a crucial part of your total energy and stamina system. As I discussed earlier, nutrient fatigue can wear you down physically and mentally as your business day progresses. This is particularly true as it pertains to weight. You have enough of a load to carry in the business world without literally carrying extra pounds of fat with you day after day.

To avoid nutrient fatigue while supercharging your body's

engine you must follow these five policies for stamina eating.

Policy 1: Eat At Least Four Times Every Day.

This policy of eating at least four times each day may sound a bit strange, especially since you may need to lose a little weight to increase stamina. Actually, this is one of the most important stamina rules. Your body needs its fuel in moderate doses throughout the day to keep energy nutrients at their optimum levels in the cells of your body. If you usually just grab a cup of coffee and juice for breakfast and don't eat lunch until 2 p.m., *you are functioning well below your peak stamina level for more than half of the day*. Your mind and body cannot function without fuel.

"But," you may say, "I'm not really hungry until later in the day. And, besides, I'm trying to save a few calories."

You definitely cannot base your body's need for stamina on your level of hunger. You must add fuel to your engine throughout the day, beginning first thing in the morning. Most people cannot judge real, physical hunger anyway. Our hunger mechanisms have been so mixed up with the psychological influences on eating that very few people know when they are hungry or just looking for something to stimulate, tranquilize or comfort them. So, forget hunger as a barometer of when it's time to eat.

Pretend your body is an automobile with a broken gas gauge. You could simply wait until you run out of gas before you fill your tank—or be more systematic about it and not run out. Many executives do the former. When they are totally fatigued they use food as a quick pick-me-up. By then it's a little late, however. During their fatigue state they might have made all kinds of faulty decisions or let important details slip because of inattention. Why not avoid the slumps? Why not make a deal with yourself that you will never run out of gas?

The best solution to your broken fuel gauge is simple: Just add gasoline at regular intervals about four or five times during the day. For your schedule, moderate intake of fuel several times a day is best because your schedule may vary. If you just fill your tank up to the top in the morning, you might still run out of fuel on busy days.

By spreading out your food intake over the day, you also are burning calories more efficiently than you would with any other food plan. My studies of metabolism to help people lose weight have verified this fact over and over again. The reason has to do with a phenomenon called *dietary thermogenesis*. Whenever you eat a meal, your body starts to burn calories at a higher than normal rate. Food actually stimulates your body's natural calorie burning process. Of course, if you eat more than your body is able to burn you'll put on weight, but if you eat four moderate-size meals a day (I'll define "moderate" in just a minute), *your metabolism will be triggered to increase its rate of burning for two to four hours after each meal*. In fact this is an excellent way to stimulate your metabolism to help you lose weight.

It is important to remember that you will have more stamina during the business day if you eat at least four and sometimes five times each day. These should be small-to-moderate size meals since large meals can make you groggy. When you eat a very large meal, your stomach and intestines receive increased blood and oxygen supplies to provide energy for digestion. Less energy is available for your muscles and brain for a short time after the meal. Moderate-size meals, particularly the ones I suggest, put less drain on your stamina.

Policy 2: Eat At Least 60% Carbohydrates, No More Than 15% Protein and No More Than 25% Fat Daily.

Earlier I discussed why glucose is an important energy source for your muscles and brain. Every day, our bodies must have an abundance of glucose derived from complex carbohydrate foods to deliver maximum energy. Most top executives know this fact well and make certain that the majority of their total daily intake comes from foods such as:

- Vegetables
- Breads
- Cereals
- Potatoes
- Pasta
- Fruit

By arranging for over half of your food to be of the complex carbohydrate variety, you are ensuring an abundance of stamina in your business, social and family life. Eat too few of these foods and you'll run out of steam early in the day.

While protein foods such as eggs, milk, cheese, chicken, beef, fish, lentils and dried beans are important nutrients, protein should constitute no more than 15% of your total daily calorie intake. In the short term, protein is not the primary energy source for your body. The idea that any amount of protein above basal metabolic need gives you super energy and strength is completely false. If you were an athlete in high school or college, you might have been taught that your body needed more protein for sports. You might even have been fed a precompetition meal of steak, chicken, fish or eggs. This meal would not have provided you with one ounce of extra strength or endurance during the sporting event. What you should have eaten (and what today's athletes eat on the day of the competition) are carbohydrates. Carbohydrates are your main stamina source. When you eat, *think carbohydrates, not protein.*

Don't get me wrong. You do need protein, but not nearly the amount that many people consume. Any extra protein you eat over your daily caloric requirements is turned into body fat. Most people don't realize that protein calories can be converted to body fat just as carbohydrate and fat calories are.

The average size adult man requires approximately 56 grams of protein per day, while an average-size woman needs approximately 46 grams. If you want to be more precise, you can calculate your protein needs by multiplying your weight in kilograms (weight in pounds divided by 2.2) by 0.8. This will give you the number of grams per day that would be considered your recommended daily allowance. Pregnant women should add 10 grams and lactating women should add 20 grams. Since there are 4 calories in each gram of protein, the average man would need only 224 calories of protein per day while the average woman would need only 184 calories.

Since most foods consist of a combination of nutrients rather than being pure protein, carbohydrate or fat, it's easier to think of your protein needs in terms of 15% of your daily caloric needs. In this way, you don't have to figure out exactly how many grams of protein are contained in a particular food.

Since an adult male with an average activity level can eat approximately 2700 calories to maintain an ideal weight, his intake of protein foods should not exceed 405 calories (for example, 7 to 8 ounces of chicken without skin—about 1½ cups, chopped). The average adult female with a moderate level of activity should eat approximately 2000 calories daily. Therefore, her consumption of protein foods should be about 300 calories.

Although fat is also an essential nutrient, only 25% of your total calories should come from fat sources. Animal fat is found in butter, whole milk, red meat and shortening.

Vegetable fat is found in margarine, oil, salad dressings, mayonnaise and nuts.

Foods high in fat not only add too many calories to our diet, but many types of fat contribute to elevated cholesterol levels. Over the years this can lead to *atherosclerosis*, a condition in which the linings of the blood vessels become clogged with fatty substances. As the blood vessels become clogged and narrowed, your risk of stroke and heart attack increases dramatically.

Fats that raise cholesterol levels are called *saturated fats*. These are found in animal products and even in some vegetable products. Many people believe that as long as a food product contains vegetable as opposed to animal fat, it is good for their health. This simply is not true. Palm oil and coconut oil, for example, have *more* saturated fat than butter! I have seen packaged foods labeled "made with 100% vegetable oil" to give you the impression that they are healthy for you. Upon closer inspection, the vegetable oil used is palm oil, one of the worst oils you can eat as far as your cholesterol is concerned. So, read labels and beware.

Avoid or limit your use of the following foods that are high in saturated fats:

- Butter
- Cream
- Shortening
- Cheese
- Coconut oil
- Whole milk
- Bacon drippings
- Palm oil
- Palm kernal oil
- Beef (particularly organ meats)

Fats that lower cholesterol are called *polyunsaturated fats*. These fats actually help your body rid itself of excessive cholesterol. Fats and oils that are high in polyunsaturates are:

- Safflower oil
- Corn oil

- Sunflower oil
- Soybean oil
- Cottonseed oil

Some vegetable oils are low in saturated fats and also low in polyunsaturated fats. These oils such as olive oil and peanut oil are called *monounsaturated fats*. While these fats were once thought to be "neutral" (that is, they neither increased nor decreased your cholesterol), recent studies indicate that monounsaturated fats *lower* total cholesterol, although not as well as polyunsaturated fats.

Fat simply is not a very efficient energy source for your body. During activities requiring stamina your body first burns carbohydrates for energy, then a combination of carbohydrates and fat, then fat and protein. Rarely in the work you do as a business executive (even on your longest and most hectic days) will you get beyond the carbohydrate burning stage. This is why eating a lot of fat and protein robs you of the stamina you need. The fat and protein calories are taking the place of valuable complex carbohydrates that your body and mind so desperately need to get you through the business day at your peak level of efficiency.

The percentages of nutrients I have given you for maximum energy should be based on total calories consumed per day. Therefore, if as a 35-year-old woman in business you are eating 1800 calories a day to maintain your weight, your nutrient breakdown should look like this:

60% Complex carbohydrates	1080 calories
15% Protein	270 calories
25% Fat	450 calories

Policy 3: Eat More High Fiber Foods.

Foods that are high in dietary fiber (your grandmother called it "roughage") must become an integral part of your nutritional program. Fiber is that part of food that is not digestible. When fiber reaches your intestines it absorbs water and swells. This results in bulky, soft stools that move more quickly through your intestinal system.

Speeding up the time between eating food and excreting the remains of that food in this way has several benefits to your health. Three of these are:

1. Less Likelihood of Constipation

If you were to eat more dietary fiber you would rarely be constipated or suffer from hemorrhoidal discomfort. If you have either of these problems, you would see dramatic improvements in as little as two to three weeks simply by eating two slices of whole wheat bread and a bowl of high fiber cereal each day.

2. Decreased Risk of Colon Cancer

Although the evidence that fiber in your diet will lessen your chances of developing cancer of the colon is not definitive, many scientists believe that fiber may provide protection in this regard. Since colon cancer can result from carcinogens produced by bacteria in the bowels, speeding the transit time of waste products in your system results in the production of less bacteria. Not only is the bacteria produced less concentrated because of the extra water absorbed by the fiber but it also has less time to act on your intestines.

3. Increased Likelihood of Weight Control

Because fiber speeds the route of foods through your body, your system will absorb fewer of the calories in those foods. Although the effects of this reduced caloric absorption on weight would be very gradual over a period of time, I'm sure you will agree that when it comes to weight control, every little bit helps.

High-fiber foods are also more filling and may help you control your appetite.

You should be on the lookout for high-fiber foods so you can add them to your diet. Some foods that qualify are the following:

HIGH-FIBER CEREALS

Many cereals are excellent sources of fiber. You must be careful of sugar in some of them, however. Recent evidence indicates that oat bran in cereals and muffins may be even better than wheat bran because it has the additional advantage of lowering blood cholesterol. Some of the best cereal choices are:

- Oat bran
- Oatmeal (choose *regular* or *quick*)
- Wheat bran
- Shredded wheat

Quaker Oats, Wheatena and Ralston Whole Wheat Cereal are excellent choices.

HIGH-FIBER BREAD AND CRACKER PRODUCTS

When choosing bread, look for those high in whole grains. The best choices are listed below. Cornbread and corn and bran muffins are at the bottom of the list because they tend to be higher in sugar and fat than the others.

- Whole wheat bread
- Rye bread
- Whole wheat matzoh
- Tacos
- Tortillas
- Stoned wheat crackers

- Whole grain melba toast
- Bran muffins
- Cornbread/corn muffins

In addition, when buying pasta make sure you choose the whole wheat varieties.

VEGETABLES AND FRUIT

Many vegetables and fruits are also high in fiber. These are your best choices:

- Broccoli
- Peas
- Corn
- Apples
- Prunes
- Carrots
- Brussels sprouts
- String beans
- Oranges
- Strawberries

Try to select these foods over others when you have the choice. It would also be quite easy for you to switch permanently to whole wheat or rye bread and to whole grain cereals. You could also buy wheat bran (the outer layers of wheat that are removed in the production of white flour). It can be purchased as miller's bran and can be added to your cereal or other foods. One to two tablespoons will give you as much fiber as you need.

The exact amount of fiber that is best for you each day has not been determined. Two tablespoons of wheat bran daily or two slices of whole wheat bread along with a high-fiber cereal daily would be sufficient.

Policy 4: Eat Refined Sugar No More Than Two to Three Times Per Week.

Sugar robs your body of its vital energy and adds only unnecessary "empty" calories. It boosts your blood sugar level only to drop it down again two to four hours later so you experience sluggishness after a brief energy "high."

I find that if you restrict yourself to no more than two or three small to moderate indulgences in sweets per week, your system can handle it. Keep in mind that there is a lot of "hidden" sugar in the foods we eat. Look at any food package and you'll see corn syrup, sucrose, fructose, molasses and honey in just about everything. This is why two to three times a week for that favorite ice cream of yours is plenty.

Some chocoholics find they must give up these sugar sources altogether. I've had good success in advising sugar lovers to eat their portions of sweets each week only under highly specific circumstances. Here are my rules to help you control your desire for sweets:

1. Eat sweets only *out of the house* (for example, in restaurants or at a friend's house).
2. Never keep sweets in the house, not even for somebody else.
3. Ask your spouse and/or family to have their sweets out of the house also.
4. Portion out your sweets and decide exactly how many or how much you are going to have before you begin eating.
5. Never, ever eat sweets (especially alone) when you are emotionally upset. Look for other ways to find relief such as exercise, relaxation or talking out your frustrations to a friend.

Policy 5: Drink More Fluids and Cut Back on Caffeine, Alcohol and Salt.

As I mentioned earlier, your body needs a proper fluid balance for you to feel vital. If you're either bloated from too much fluid or dehydrated from too little fluid, you won't feel very energetic.

Drinking four to six glasses of water or other noncaffeinated beverage during the day is essential. While you don't have to eliminate caffeine and alcohol from your diet, you should restrict them to the amounts I describe in my meal plans in Chapter 7.

Salt is associated with both high blood pressure and excessive fluid retention. It is generally a good idea for everyone to reduce salt intake. I find that a great many people are getting this message. More and more executives who come to my Institute on Hilton Head have already given up salt.

The easiest guideline I can give you for how much salt you should use is simply to tell you not to add salt to your food in cooking or at the table. Your goal is to reduce your sodium intake to 2000 mg, which is about one teaspoon of table salt. Because most packaged foods contain salt and since you will be eating in restaurants that add salt to your food, you do not need to add any at all. Even though you're not using a salt shaker, you'll still be getting about 2000 mg per day. This is not bad if you consider that many people eat between 5000 and 10,000 mg of salt each day without even realizing it!

In this era of hypertensive executives it is also becoming much more acceptable to order salt-free food in restaurants. Just tell the waiter you are on a low sodium diet and ask that your food be prepared without salt as a seasoning.

Many executives ask me about salt substitutes. These products are mostly potassium chloride. While extra potassium won't hurt you, you are getting more than enough naturally on my food plan through fruits and potatoes. I recommend against these substitutes because you're just avoiding the issue by using them. Simply give up the salt altogether and you'll get used to it in about two weeks. If your food tastes a little bland at first, add a few fresh herbs or use one of the bottled herbal mixtures that are currently on the market. Salt actually masks the real flavor of foods; you will come to enjoy their true tastes.

6

▼

A Simple Guide for Breakfast, Lunch and Dinner

Through a great deal of personal research I have simplified my food plan for you so you will get a stamina-enhancing nutritional system that is both well-balanced and easy to live with. You can modify the program's guidelines depending on your day's schedule in the business world.

I want this nutrition system to fit into your life, not cause you to adapt your schedule to the system. Otherwise, you might be able to follow this meal plan for a while, but it would surely break down as changes occur in your schedule. Also, I don't want to give you a plan for the next week or the next month, but for the rest of your life. Unless these stamina policies can fit easily into your life, you'll never accomplish what I know you can accomplish. I know you can develop the stamina you should have so you can lead the kind of life you were meant to live.

My basic stamina food plan begins with the types of

foods you should eat at dinner each evening throughout the week.

Starting Your food Plan: Dinners

Before you think of any other meal in the day, plan the *main course* for your dinner meal. Don't worry about what else might accompany the meal right now. We only need to plan the main course for dinner each day of the week. In order to end up with the proper nutritional ratios for maximum stamina, you must ensure that you follow my 2-2-2-1 dinner food plan. Make sure your 7 dinner meals during the week follow this pattern:

MY 2-2-2-1 DINNER FOOD PLAN

- Poultry—Any 2 evenings
- Pasta or vegetable dish—Any 2 evenings
- Fish or shellfish—Any 2 evenings
- Lean red meat*—Any 1 evening

*Note: You may modify the 2-2-2-1 plan by choosing not to eat any red meat at all. It would be quite easy for you to skip the red meat and substitute pasta or a vegetable dish for that meal.

An alternative way to think about the 2-2-2-1 plan is as follows:

Dinner Rule: Do Not Eat Red Meat More Than One Evening Per Week

OPTIONS: Plan a poultry dinner for two evenings, a pasta or vegetable dish for two evenings, fish or shellfish for two evenings and a lean red meat for one evening.

or

Schedule a poultry dinner for two evenings, a pasta or vegetable dish for three evenings, fish or shellfish for two evenings and omit the red meat completely.

The order in which these food choices occur each week is not important. For example, you might choose to have spaghetti on Sunday, broiled chicken on Monday, shrimp or lobster on Tuesday, filet mignon on Wednesday, lasagna on Thursday, broiled flounder on Friday and a small cornish hen on Saturday.

Don't worry about quantities and portion sizes right now. Your caloric needs will vary depending on whether you are a man or a woman and on whether you are trying to lose weight. I'll give you complete specifications in the next chapter when I discuss the stamina eating plans.

Just remember to follow the 2-2-2-1 pattern. The sequence is completely up to you. You should try to plan the dinner meals for the week in advance, perhaps on a Sunday night when you're looking over your schedule for the next week. You might even jot down in your appointment book which main course you will be aiming for each night. This way, if you are dining out with business associates, you'll know exactly what to order. I understand that sometimes you may be at a convention or benefit banquet and not know ahead of time what will be served. If at all possible, try to find out so that you can shift foods around the rest of the week. When in doubt, try to get your pasta/vegetable and fish dinner meals in early in the week since it's almost a sure bet these items won't be served at a banquet or convention dinner. You are more likely to have chicken or beef.

Before I discuss portion sizes and the foods that you will be eating along with the main courses, let's first discuss breakfasts, lunches and the stamina snack. As you can see, I am building a system for you one step at a time. When I'm finished you'll have a complete outline of an easy-to-follow food plan designed to keep you healthy and full of energy and stamina.

The Next Step: Lunches

Since we are working backward through your meals each day, let's examine next what you might choose for lunch. The seven lunches during the week should be divided as follows:

Any four days—Meatless meals
Any three days—poultry, fish or lean beef

By meatless four times a week, I am referring to such meals as:

• Soup and salad
• Fruit plate
• Pasta primavera
• Vegetable plate
• Baked potato stuffed
  with cheese/vegetables
• Selective salad bar*

*Note: You must be aware of the many "calorie hazards" in salad bars. Avoid chicken, tuna and pasta salads and cole slaw because they are full of fatty mayonnaise. Bacon bits are high in fat and sodium. Keep away from marinated items because of their high sodium content. Choose items such as lettuce, carrots, beets, spinach, mushrooms, bean sprouts, or three bean salad. Also, choose low calorie dressings or simply use a little lemon and vinegar.

Since these lunches are meatless, avoid tuna, shrimp, crabmeat, chicken or turkey salads if they are offered on the salad bar. Any form of eggs such as an omelette or quiche would be considered a red meat, so do not eat eggs for lunch on the same day you are eating red meat for dinner.

Lunch Rule : Do Not Eat Poultry, Fish or Lean Beef at More Than Three Lunches Per Week.

OPTIONS: Plan a meatless lunch four days a week, and a poultry, fish or lean beef lunch on the three remaining days.

or

Plan a meatless lunch four days a week and poultry or fish on the three remaining days, omitting the lean beef choice.

or

Plan a meatless lunch seven days a week.

Lunch Rule 2: Do Not Eat Poultry, Fish or Beef at Lunch on the Same Day You Are Having Poultry, Fish or Lean Beef at Dinner More Than One Time Per Week Only.

OPTIONS: Schedule two of your three meat lunches on days when you are having a meatless dinner such as pasta or vegetables.

or

Schedule only two meat lunches per week but

make certain they are on days when you are having a meatless dinner.

or

Schedule meatless lunches seven days per week.

Lunch Rule 3: Never Schedule Red Meat (Such As Steak, Veal Or Lamb Chops) For Lunch On Days When You Will Be Having Red Meat For Dinner.

The Final Step: Breakfasts

Breakfasts are relatively simple on this plan since I find that most people in the business world are satisfied with an easy-to-prepare breakfast. For your seven breakfasts each week, you should plan a cereal/bread/fruit combination on five days with the option of having an egg/bread/fruit combination on the two remaining days.

You may choose to schedule the cereal/bread/fruit for all seven days and omit the eggs altogether. Just be certain you do not eat eggs more than two mornings per week.

Breakfast Rule: Do Not Eat Eggs More Than Two Mornings Per Week.

OPTIONS: Plan a cereal/bread/fruit breakfast five days a week and an egg/bread/fruit combination on two remaining days.

or

Schedule cereal/bread/fruit for *all* seven days and omit the eggs completely.

My Weekly Meal Planning Chart

To simplify these breakfast, lunch and dinner choices, I have devised a meal planning chart for you to follow. I suggest you write this chart out and keep it in your wallet. Many of my executives keep this chart in the small appointment book they carry around with them. Whether you are in a restaurant, at home or on a trip, all you have to do is refer to the meal planning chart and you'll know exactly what to order for your meals on any given days.

	Weekly Meal Planning Chart						
	Any day	Any day	Any day	Any day	Any day	Any day	Any day
Breakfast	C/B/F	C/B/F	E/B/F	C/B/F	C/B/F	E/B/F	C/B/F
Lunch	Po/Fi	ML	ML	RM	Po	ML	ML
Dinner	Pa/V	Fi	Po	Pa/V	Fi	Po	RM

Chart Abbreviations

C/B/F = Cereal/Bread/Fruit
E/B/F = Egg/Bread/Fruit
Po = Poultry
Fi = Fish
ML = Meatless
RM = Red meat
Pa = Pasta
V = Vegetable

Note: As I mentioned previously, if you choose not to eat red meat at all, you can substitute pasta or a vegetable dish for that meal.

The Stamina Snack

To keep your engine going strong, it is essential for you to have a fourth meal every day in addition to breakfast, lunch and dinner. This "meal" is actually a snack—*the stamina snack*. The stamina snack is part of my *resting-in-motion* revitalization routine described in Chapter 10. It must also be part of your daily meal plan. Since eating times should be spread out during the day and since most executives eat dinner rather late, you should plan to eat your stamina snack late in the afternoon—this is when most people experience a slump in energy and need refueling.

I will describe this snack in detail in a later chapter. All you need to remember now is that it consists of 16 ounces of cold sparkling water and one piece of high energy/high potassium fruit such as a whole banana or an orange.

Be sure to schedule this late afternoon snack every day or you may run out of the fuel your body needs to keep you on top. If you know you will be having a very late lunch on a particular day, schedule the stamina snack between breakfast and lunch.

Now that you know the type of food that should make up the main course of each meal during the week, what about portion sizes? What types and amounts of side dishes such as vegetables, potatoes, rice and dinner salads should you have? The executive stamina eating plans outlined in the next chapter will give you all the details.

7

▼

Stamina Food Choices Made Easy

The portion size and variety of food choices on the Hilton Head executive stamina eating plan depends on who you are and what you weigh. Due to differences in metabolism, for example, older people need less food than younger ones, and women should eat less than men since women have lower rates of metabolism than men. Portion size and calories are also related to your level of physical activity.

I have devised three basic portion plans for your own particular needs. These include:

Food plan 1—Male maintenance plan
Food plan 2—Female maintenance plan
Food plan 3—Weight loss plan

Since a man's metabolic rate is higher than a woman's, the male maintenance plan allows between 2400 and 2600 calories while the female maintenance plan allows between

1800 and 2000 calories. The weight loss plan for men or women allows approximately 1000 calories, although calories are increased to 1250 every third week. As I pointed out in my book, *The Hilton Head Metabolism Diet*, varying calories during a diet is essential to setting and maintaining a strong metabolism. Slight, periodic increases in calories during a diet actually *boost* your metabolism and *lead to a more consistent weight loss in the long run*. If you keep the same low calorie rate week after week, your body thinks you're starving and tries to conserve energy by *lowering* your metabolism, resulting in slower weight loss. This is the last thing you want to happen!

Each of these food plans follows the basic structure of the main meal choices I have outlined in Chapter 6. All of the plans control total food intake in terms of *portions* rather than calories. I don't want you to have to bother with calorie counting. What follows are guidelines on the general types of foods to eat along with approximate portion sizes for each of the three food plans.

Food Plan 1: Male Maintenance

BREAKFAST

Cereal (low sugar type/ no sugar added)	1½ cups
Milk (low fat/skim)	1 cup
Bread/roll/muffin (whole wheat/rye)	1
Margarine	1 teaspoon
Fruit juice (unsweetened)	½ cup

| Fruit | 1 piece or ½ cup (melon would be ⅛ piece) |
| Eggs (poached or boiled only)* | 2 |

*If you choose to eat eggs for breakfast, have them only twice a week. Omit cereal and milk on egg days.

| Coffee or tea* | 1 or 2 cups (a cup being about one measuring cup) |

*Restrict caffeinated coffee or tea to no more than 2 times per day. Otherwise, drink decaffeinated coffee or herbal tea.

LUNCH

Depending on the appropriate main course choice from the weekly meal planning chart, your lunch choices might include one of any of the following (remember, these are only suggestions and any choices that follow my guidelines are okay):

Soup/Salad (Avoid cream soups; order salad dressing on the side and use only 2 tablespoons)

Fruit/Cottage cheese plate

Vegetable quiche/Salad (Do not order quiche if you had egg for breakfast)

Fruit/Yogurt

Pasta salad/Bread/Margarine

Sliced chicken/turkey sandwich on whole wheat or rye

Cheese/Vegetable omelet (Not on egg breakfast days)

Lean roast beef on rye with potato salad

Poultry (4–5 oz), vegetable, potato (baked or boiled only) or rice, fresh fruit (avoid canned, syrupy variety)

Fish (6–8 oz), vegetable, potato (baked or boiled only) or rice, fresh fruit

Pork chop, lamb chop, veal or small steak with salad, vegetable, potato/rice

Decaffeinated coffee or tea

STAMINA SNACK*

Sparkling water   16 oz
(Served cold with
   ice)

Fruit   1 piece

*Refer to Chapter 11 for the list of fruits that I suggest for this particular meal and more about including the stamina snack in your schedule.

DINNER

Depending on the main course choices from my weekly meal planning chart, these are the approximate portions you should choose:

Either:

Poultry	5–8 oz
Fish/Shellfish	6–10 oz
Red meat (beef, lamb, veal, pork)	4–6 oz
Pasta (any style but must be meatless)	1–2 cups

Served with:

Soup (avoid cream soup)	1 cup
Salad	1 serving
Vegetable	1 cup
Potato (baked/boiled)	1 whole
or rice	½ cup
Bread/roll	1 or 2
Margarine	1 tablespoon
Fresh fruit	1 piece or ½ cup
Decaffeinated coffee or tea	1 or 2 cups

OPTIONAL FOODS FOR MEALS OR AS SEPARATE SNACK

Depending on your level of exercise and individual metabolism you may be able to eat additional foods, snack foods or even occasional sweet foods without any negative effects on your stamina or your weight. Here are some suggestions for these extras:

Fresh fruit (1 to 2 pieces)

Bagel (1) with cream cheese (1 oz)

Popcorn, air popped, no butter (4 cups)

Wheat crackers (6) with low-fat cheese (1 oz)

Raw vegetables (1 cup, chopped; avoid dips)

Yogurt (8-oz container of plain with ¼ cup fresh fruit, e.g., blueberries, added)

Nuts, dry roasted, unsalted (½ cup)

Sweets:*

Ice cream (½ cup)

Sherbet (½ cup)

Cookies (3 to 4 small)

Candy (1 oz)

Cake/Pie (⅛ of 9-in. cake or pie)

*Note: No more than three sweets (in the portions listed above) per week and never within four hours prior to an important business meeting.

ALCOHOL

Unless you have a problem with alcohol, moderate alcohol consumption should not affect your overall stamina. Avoid alcohol during travel and before any important or particularly long business meetings, however. Alcohol robs your body of fluid and, because it is chemically a sugar, it may quickly raise and then lower your blood sugar level, leaving you fatigued. Alcohol is also a nutrient robber, particularly of thiamine and niacin, which we need for energy production and metabolic activity.

I strongly recommend that you not exceed two *standard equivalent* drinks in any one day. *One* standard equivalent drink is defined as either:

> 1½ oz of liquor (80 proof)
> 1 12-oz beer
> 4–6 oz of wine

If you are at a cocktail party or business convention and overdo it a bit, don't drink alcohol at all the next evening. In fact, some executives choose to drink alcohol only on weekends, keeping their minds completely clear during the week. The cocktail you have when you get home may relax you, but it also may interfere with the stamina you need for activities with your spouse or family. A mixture of two parts fruit juice to one part carbonated water, mixed with ice and preceded or followed by a 30-minute walk will relax and refresh you at the end of a busy day like no alcoholic beverage can.

Food Plan 2: Female Maintenance

BREAKFAST

Cereal*	1 cup
Milk (low fat/skim)	1 cup
Bread/roll/muffin (whole wheat/rye)	1
Margarine	1 teaspoon

Either:

Fruit juice (unsweetened)	¼ cup

or

Fruit	½ piece or ¼ cup (melon would be ⅛ piece)
Egg (poached or boiled only)	1

*Omit cereal on egg days but include everything else, even milk.

Coffee or tea	1 cup

LUNCH

(same as the male maintenance plan)

STAMINA SNACK

(same as the male maintenance plan)

DINNER

Depending on the main course choices from my weekly meal planning chart, these are the approximate portions you should choose:

Either:

Poultry	4–7 oz
Fish/Shellfish	5–9 oz
Red Meat (beef, lamb, veal, pork)	3–5 oz
Pasta (any style)	6–8 oz

Served with:

Soup (avoid cream soups)	1 cup (as opposed to 1 bowl)
Salad (with low calorie dressing or lemon/vinegar)	1 serving
Vegetable	½ cup
Potato/Rice	1 whole/½ cup
Bread/Roll	1
Margarine	1 teaspoon
Fruit	1 piece or ½ cup
Coffee/Tea	1 cup

Optional Foods for Meals or As Separate Snack

Depending on your level of exercise and individual metabolism, you may be able to eat additional foods, snack foods or even occasional sweet foods without any negative effects on your stamina or your weight. Many women, however, find that their body weight is very sensitive to what they eat each day and they must keep a close watch on their food habits. In addition, some people have a particular problem with sweets. In that case, you might be better off sticking to the three meals and snack already described and forgetting about any other food. Otherwise, here are some suggestions for these extras:

Fresh fruit (1 piece)

Bagel (1) with cream cheese (½ oz)

Popcorn, air popped, no butter (4 cups)

Wheat crackers (6) with low-fat cheese (1 oz)

Raw vegetables (1 cup, chopped, avoid dips)

Yogurt (4-oz plain with fresh fruit, e.g., blueberries, added)

Nuts, dry roasted, unsalted (¼ cup)

Sweets:*

　Ice cream (½ cup)

　Sherbet (½ cup)

　Cookies (3 to 4 small)

　Candy (1 oz)

　Cake/Pie (⅛ of 9-in. cake or pie)

*Note: No more than two sweets (in the portions listed above) per week and never within four hours prior to an important business meeting.

ALCOHOL

(same as the male maintenance plan)

Food Plan 3: Weight Control (Male or Female)

BREAKFAST

Cereal	¾ cup
Milk (low fat/skim)	½ cup
Bread (whole wheat or diet bread)	1
Fruit	½ piece or ¼ cup (melon would be ⅛ piece)

LUNCH

Depending on the appropriate main course choice from my weekly meal planning chart, your lunch would include one of the following:

Salad or selective salad bar (Use 2 to 3 tablespoons of diet dressing, served on the side, if possible, or use lemon/vinegar only.)

Fruit/Cottage cheese plate (Eat no more than ¼ cup of cottage cheese.)

Vegetable Quiche/Salad (Use diet dressing served on the side, if possible, or lemon/vinegar only.)

Shrimp cocktail (Eat the shrimp only and forego the cocktail sauce.)

Lean roast beef on rye (no mayonnaise)

Poultry (2–4 oz), Vegetable, ½ Baked Potato/¼ cup Rice (no margarine)

Fish (4–6 oz), Vegetable, ½ Baked Potato/¼ cup Rice
(no margarine)

STAMINA SNACK

(same as the male and female maintenance plans)

DINNER

Depending on the main course choices from my weekly
meal planning chart, these are the approximate portions you
should choose:

Either:

Poultry*	3–6 oz
Fish/Shellfish*	4–8 oz
Red meat (beef, lamb, veal, pork)*	3–4 oz
Pasta (either garnished only with Parmesan or served with sauce on the side, used sparingly)	½ cup

*All meats broiled or baked with no sauce or gravy

Served with:

Salad (diet dressing or lemon/vinegar)	1 serving
Vegetable (no butter or sauce)	½ cup
Potato/Rice	½/¼ cup
Margarine	½ teaspoon

Fruit	½ piece/¼ cup
Coffee or Tea	1 cup

OPTIONAL FOODS AND ALCOHOL

No optional foods or alcohol are included in the weight control plan.

THE THIRD WEEK BOOSTER

In order to keep your metabolism strong while you are trying to lose weight, you must increase calories slightly *every third week*. This is particularly true if you have a great deal of weight to lose and must stay on my weight control plan for a while.

Every third week of your meal plan you must increase your calories by 250 each day. You can do this by simply adding an extra piece of bread and fruit and an extra ounce of fish or poultry whenever they are called for in your meal plan. Another way to increase calories is to add a second snack each day (perhaps in the evening) of fruit and bread, air-popped popcorn, or even cereal, milk and fruit. After this booster week is over, return to the regular Weight Control Plan for two more weeks. Keep alternating until you have reached your desired weight.

If you feel a need for a more detailed, low-calorie diet plan, I suggest you consult my previous book, *The Hilton Head Metabolism Diet*.

Once you have lost your weight, switch to either the male or the female maintenance plans.

Best Bets for Food Preparation

With any of my food plans you will need to make healthy choices not only in terms of *what* you are eating but in *how* it is prepared. This is a little tricky when eating at restaurants or banquets since you are not always certain of the food preparation methods used. For example, you might not know whether the vegetables are fresh, frozen or canned. For this reason I will give you my "Best Choices Lists" for eating in restaurants, banquets and buffets in the next chapter.

Here are some overall best bets to get you started.

1. Choose meats with little marbling (*marbling* describes the network of white lines—fat—running through the meat).

2. Prior to cooking, trim all visible fat from meats.

3. Always remove skin from poultry *before* cooking if possible and never eat poultry skin that is served to you.

4. Never prepare or eat fried foods.

5. Eat foods that are baked, broiled, boiled or roasted, preferably on a rack so that excess fat has been allowed to drain off.

6. Eat fresh or frozen vegetables as opposed to the canned ones that are full of salt.

7. Use polyunsaturated or monounsaturated vegetable oils and polyunsaturated margarines; don't use butter and saturated oils.

8. Drink low-fat or skim milk and avoid whole milk.

9. Eat low-fat cheeses that are labeled as containing not more than two grams of fat per ounce.

10. Choose whole grain cereals such as shredded wheat and avoid cereals with sugar added.

11. Eat whole grain breads such as whole wheat, rye and pumpernickel and avoid white breads, rolls and buttery breads such as croissants.

12. Avoid casseroles, since they can be high in fat and contain high calorie ingredients.

13. Eat foods without sauces, butter and salt.

14. Eat the skins of fruits and potatoes to add more fiber to your diet.

15. Avoid creamy or "chunky" soups and stews which are high in fat and may contain large amounts of red meat.

16. Choose low-fat luncheon meats (with labels showing no more than two grams of fat per ounce) such as turkey, chicken or lean boiled ham.

17. Avoid high-fat meats such as corned beef, pastrami, spare ribs, frankfurters, ground beef containing more than 15% fat, sausage, bacon and high-fat luncheon meats such as bologna, most ham and salami.

18. Avoid catsup and mustard since they are high in sugar and salt.

In the next chapter, you will find specific guidelines for those business situations in which you have little or no control over food choices or food preparation.

8

▼

Easy Stamina Eating for Every Business Event

A s an executive you are faced with just about every difficult eating situation that exists. You must travel, attend business lunches, meet associates for breakfast meetings and attend banquets of every description.

Let me assure you that in spite of the difficulties these business events present as far as stamina eating is concerned, I will give you easy-to-follow guidelines so that *no business eating situation will be troublesome for you*. Since business schedules are often erratic, you may have little time to plan a strategy for food choices at a particular business event. Without guidelines and practice you may find the situation overwhelming, in addition to the fact that you may have to concentrate more on the business at hand than on proper nutrition. Under these circumstances you may simply eat whatever is available, healthy or not. The trouble is that these wrong choices will reduce your energy, stamina and concentration as the day progresses.

Below are some simple but effective rules to follow in

every business event to help you follow my stamina eating plan. The more you put them into practice, the more you'll be able to handle these events with ease. In no time, you will be making the correct choices with little thought or effort. Executives who have learned my system at the Hilton Head Health Institute report that the correct food choices become second nature to them within a very short period of time. With their new-found stamina and newly acquired nutritional skills, they can focus 100% effort where it should be: on the business at hand.

Stamina Eating and Your Corporate Image

The way you portray yourself to others is obviously a big part of your corporate world: You must project an image of confidence, efficiency and success. By using this program, you also will be conveying the image of a healthy executive who never seems to tire. Unfortunately, to some, the image of a powerful executive is associated with the hearty eater who orders a 16-ounce sirloin and two double martinis for lunch while encouraging his business colleagues to do the same.

But there is a new breed of super-executives who pride themselves on health and stamina. The successful manager's image is rapidly changing and you must change to keep up with the times. For example, it has become fashionable for New York executives to meet one another for tea in the late afternoon. In some circles, this routine is rapidly replacing the traditional cocktail hour. Years ago such behavior would have resulted in a "wimp" image and may have had detrimental effects on business relationships. Not so anymore.

Today, ordering healthy foods such as a salad instead of a steak for lunch is much more acceptable; in fact, it shows that you are on the cutting edge when it comes to keeping in peak form. You can build a powerful corporate image around a successful/healthy lifestyle in which low-calorie, low-fat food choices are the norm. In the long run, this nutritional plan will make you a sharp, successful manager whom others will want to emulate.

Even if you are hosting a business lunch for others whom you are trying to impress, you should feel free to order whatever you like. Never give up your stamina eating program simply because you feel you are making others uncomfortable. Most people care very little about what you are ordering. If they are feeling uncomfortable because they are eating a high calorie meal, that's their problem, not yours. *You* are not making them feel uncomfortable or guilty; they are making themselves feel that way. Would you eat something that you are deathly allergic to simply to please a client? Of course not. So make your own choices and let others judge you on your business efficiency and stamina and not your eating habits.

Women executives often have special problems with image that I will be discussing in Chapter 16. One of the most successful graduates of my Institute is Trudy, a political consultant from the Midwest. During one of our follow-up contacts with her, Trudy described how she dealt with just such a problem at a business lunch:

"Last week I was at a luncheon meeting with four very influential political analysts. I was hosting, so I let each of them order first. Each ordered choices from the menu that were very heavy, high-calorie, high-fat meals. When it came to me, I hesitated for a minute, thinking about how I used to respond in this situation before the Hilton Head Executive Stamina Program. In the past I would have felt intimidated and ordered something like a steak with French fries to be 'one of the boys.' I didn't want to present the image of a compulsive woman who is more concerned with dieting than politics.

"Well, the 'new' me is different. I ordered a large salad with the dressing on the side so I could control the amount. I did this in a very matter-of-fact manner and then immediately entered into a discussion of a rather complex political issue, giving my opinions in a concise and well-conceptualized manner. I find that if I order with as little fuss and fanfare as possible and if I put the emphasis of the lunch on business rather than what everyone is eating, I feel very positive about the image I am portraying.

"In fact, if I get any comments about my food choices they usually indicate that I am viewed as a strong, in-control professional. For example, after the lunch last week, one of the analysts commented, 'I sure wish I had your willpower. You always seem to handle these situations so well. I really shouldn't have had that eclair for dessert but I'm just so weak when it comes to sweets.' *I* was being viewed as the strong one in the group."

Now let's get down to my stamina eating guidelines for every business event. I'm sure you realize that in most cases there is no *one* right way to handle these situations but, rather, there are various choices you can make. That's why I'm giving you my best choices for a variety of business events.

The Best Choices Lists

Stamina Eating at Breakfast Meetings

1. If you are able to choose from a menu, order the cereal/bread/fruit or egg/bread/fruit combinations in accordance with my breakfast rules in Chapters 6 and 7.

2. Order high-fiber, low-sugar cereals such as Shredded Wheat, All Bran, 40% Bran or oatmeal.

3. If cereal is not available, order an extra piece of whole wheat, rye or pumpernickel bread.

4. If whole wheat, rye or pumpernickel are not available, choose an English muffin, roll, bagel or white bread but avoid croissants, doughnuts and Danish.

5. Use margarine if you wish, but avoid butter, jelly and preserves.

6. Avoid pancakes, waffles and French toast.

7. If fresh fruit is not available, order fruit juice instead.

8. If you cannot get your egg poached or boiled, skip the egg and order the cereal/bread/fruit breakfast instead.

9. If you cannot order from a menu and the same meal is served to everyone, avoid fried or scrambled eggs, bacon, sausage, and croissants (these are all loaded with fat or butter). In this situation have orange juice and unbuttered toast. If anyone comments on this, simply say that you aren't one for eating large breakfasts, and change the subject.

10. If the toast is already buttered ask the waiter or waitress for dry toast.

11. If nothing seems appropriate, drink two glasses of orange juice and have a piece of fresh fruit after the breakfast meeting is over. It's a good idea to keep an orange or banana in your briefcase at all times.

12. If you are scheduled for an early morning meeting and breakfast will not be served, always make sure you get up early and eat before the meeting.

Stamina Eating at Restaurant Luncheon and Dinner Meetings: Reading Between the Menu's Lines

1. When ordering pasta, stay away from selections with meat sauce, cream sauce (such as fettucine Alfredo), butter and olive oil. Some of your best pasta choices are:

> Pasta primavera
> Pasta with red clam sauce
> Baked ziti (meatless)
> Spaghetti marinara
> Eggplant lasagna

2. When ordering fish, choose non-shellfish over shellfish. Shellfish are not considered as taboo in regard to cholesterol as they once were. If you order shellfish your first choice should be lobster, then crab and then shrimp (which is the highest of the three in cholesterol).

3. Avoid oil-packed tuna, canned salmon, red sockeye salmon and mackerel (all are high in fat).

4. Your best fish choices are:

> Dover sole with crabmeat
> Flounder, red snapper, bass, haddock, cod,
> perch, halibut or sole—grilled, baked,
> poached, steamed or broiled without butter
> Lobster tails
> Flounder stuffed with crabmeat
> Fresh river trout served on a bed of rice

5. When ordering poultry, avoid duck and goose (their all-dark meat is very fatty), stews, creamy or cheese sauces. Always remove the skin before eating.

Your best choices are:

Cornish game hen
Chicken with snow peas
Chicken piccata
Coq au vin
Herbal chicken
Breast of chicken Florentine

6. When ordering red meat, avoid heavy sauces such as Béarnaise and remove all visible fat before eating. Decline rib roast, brisket of beef, short ribs, spareribs, sausage, frankfurters and corned beef.

Your best red meat choices are:

Filet mignon
Extra-lean ground beef
Pot roast (heel of round)
Veal scaloppine Marsala
Osso buco
Roast leg of lamb
Pork chops

7. If you are ordering a light lunch or if nothing on the dinner menu looks appropriate and you are ordering two appetizers or an appetizer and a salad, here are some best choices:

Fresh fruit plate with cottage cheese
Dinner salad (add lemon or ask for dressing on the side)
with shrimp cocktail (no sauce)
Spinach salad (no bacon)
Oysters Rockefeller, tossed salad, rolls
Mussels marinara, rolls, fresh fruits in season
Tomato soup and tossed salad
Vegetable soup with bread sticks
Crudités, crab claws, rolls
Sliced chicken/turkey sandwich on whole wheat bread

Vegetable plate
Baked potato stuffed with cheese/broccoli

8. The American Heart Association has a new program called "Eating Away from Home" which helps restaurants and hotels develop menu items that are low in fat, calories, and cholesterol. If you are in a participating hotel restaurant such as Hyatt, Sheraton, Stouffer, Hilton, Radisson or Marriott, ask for their "light" menu and make your choices from it. Better yet, call your local American Heart Association chapter for a list of all the restaurants in your city that are cooperating in this program and plan your business lunches and dinners at those restaurants.

Stamina Eating at Banquets Where No Choice Is Available

1. If there is a salad, eat it with a small amount of dressing (avoid the creamy ones) or lemon (you may have to ask for this).

2. If an appetizer is served and it is appropriate (such as shrimp cocktail) eat it. If it is not appropriate, push it to the side or ask the waiter or waitress not to serve it to you.

3. In case the entrée is not a good choice, take two rolls and several crudités and put them on your bread plate, in case you need them later.

4. Avoid entrées that are not appropriate for your stamina eating plan (for example, beef when you've already had your allotment of beef for that week) or when it is high in calories or fat such as creamed chicken.

5. Try to modify the entrée to make it more acceptable: You might scrape off the Béarnaise sauce, the melted cheese or the breading.

6. If the entrée cannot be modified, leave it and eat the vegetables (as long as they are baked or boiled).

7. If just about everything is inappropriate, eat a small amount of the most acceptable items or just eat your salad and rolls.

8. As soon as you are finished with what you have chosen to eat, have your plate removed if this seems appropriate.

9. If you know ahead of time what will be served at the banquet and it does not seem appropriate, eat your meal before you go and arrive late, just in time for coffee. If you must be present for meals, eat beforehand anyway and eat little or nothing at the banquet. If anyone asks why you're eating so little, you might say that you had a large, late lunch and aren't hungry.

Stamina Eating at Buffets
(When There Are Too Many Choices)

1. Look over the buffet carefully, planning your strategy *before* you get in line. Once a food choice is on your plate, it's there to tempt you throughout your meal.

2. Take your time and try to be one of the last ones going through the buffet.

3. Eat slowly so you won't be tempted to go back for seconds. A good rule of thumb: Spend more time talking than eating.

4. Choose a plain, simple entrée without butter or sauces.

5. Avoid foods that might be high in fat or calories, such as fried foods or casseroles.

6. If none of the entrées is appropriate, load up on salad, vegetables (without sauce or butter) and rolls.

7. If nothing is low calorie or low fat, choose small portions of what is best.

8. If your host urges you to try more, refuse politely and compliment him or her on a delicious meal. Be direct and avoid such comments as "Well, I really shouldn't," or

"I'm not supposed to." Say something like, "No thank you. The meal was delicious and I am full."

Stamina Eating at Coffee Breaks

1. Instead of drinking coffee, have my Power Snack (a mixture of orange juice and carbonated water described in Chapter 11) or carbonated water alone, or a noncaffeinated, low-calorie soft drink. Bottled carbonated fruit drinks are fine as long as they do not contain sugar.

2. Avoid sugary snacks like Danish or doughnuts.

3. If sweet snacks are routinely available in the office for coffee breaks, avoid the area where they are kept. Better yet, if you have any say-so, try to have these snacks eliminated and replaced with fresh fruit.

4. Take your break a little earlier or later than everyone else so you won't be as exposed to others eating tempting foods.

5. Use your coffee break as a time for a walk outside or up and down the stairs, or better yet, for my resting-in-motion routine described in Chapter 11.

Stamina Eating During the Cocktail Hour

1. Arrive late so you won't be exposed for hours to the temptation of alcohol and hors d'oeuvres.

2. Even if you are going to be drinking alcohol, make your first drink a nonalcoholic one. This will slow your pace, since the first drink at a cocktail party is usually consumed at a faster rate than subsequent drinks. The more the alcohol affects you, the more likely you'll give in to tempting high-calorie foods.

3. As a standard procedure, make every other drink a nonalcoholic one.

4. If you are discussing business or will be doing business after the party, drink *only* nonalcoholic beverages such as juice, juice and carbonated water or club soda by itself.

5. Don't make excuses for not drinking alcohol. It is your choice and you don't need to give anyone any reason for it.

6. Ignore chips, dips, canapés and other high-fat, high-salt and high-calorie foods.

7. If you choose to eat something, nibble on a few raw vegetables.

8. Stand away from the hors d'oeuvres table, preferably with your back to it.

9. Remind yourself that just because food is being served, you do not have to eat it.

10. Focus your attention on people and conversation rather than food and drink.

11. Eat your stamina snack before you go to the cocktail party so you won't be hungry for hors d'oeuvres.

9

▼

Avoiding Overdoses of Vitamin and Mineral Supplements

Most people have the erroneous notion that doses of certain vitamins and minerals above the recommended daily allowance will enhance energy and stamina. Well, *nothing could be further from the truth*.

While many nutritionists and athletic trainers may espouse the "megavitamin theory" of stamina, there is no scientific support for this notion. The bulk of scientific evidence shows that for healthy people megadoses of vitamins and minerals have *no beneficial effect* on energy level, and the vast majority of health professionals know this. This fact is proven, and any scientifically minded professional will tell you the same thing.

So why is there any controversy at all? One reason may be that the vitamin and mineral industry is a $5-billion-a-year business. Moreover, almost 40% of adult Americans are thought to be taking megavitamin supplements of one kind or another, and believe that megavitamins are helping them feel better. Well, if what I have to say is unpopular, so be it.

The reason I'm so concerned about vitamin overdoses is that, contrary to popular belief, they can be harmful. In fact, they can be *very* harmful to your overall health.

First of all, let me say that we all certainly need vitamins and minerals. If you are eating a variety of healthy foods such as those in the Hilton Head plan, however, and if your doctor has found no problems such as anemia or other deficiency, you are getting all of the vitamins and minerals you need (with only two possible exceptions for women, which I will discuss in a later chapter). Even if you were not eating a well-rounded diet or were on a restricted calorie diet, you could make sure you were getting adequate nutrition simply by taking a multivitamin with a mineral supplement.

You must understand that aside from the two exceptions I will discuss for women, all you need are the recommended daily allowances (RDA) for vitamins and minerals. If you follow my Hilton Head plan, the chances are you can obtain sufficient vitamins and minerals from your daily diet. Extra doses do you no good at all. Actually, vitamins contain no usable energy. Once your minimum requirement is met, extra doses of some vitamins are simply stored for future use or, in the case of the so-called water soluable vitamins, are excreted from the body.

It is also important to remember that the RDAs provided by the scientific community are actually much higher than the average person's minimum daily requirements. So you're getting more than enough anyway.

It really takes very little food to satisfy your vitamin/mineral requirements. For example, any one of the following will more than satisfy your daily requirements for vitamin C: six ounces of orange juice, two medium tomatoes, one baked potato, or one stalk of broccoli, not overcooked. And these are only a few of the foods that could provide your vitamin C needs.

What worries me most about the popularity of megadoses

of vitamins is that this purely superstitious behavior takes the emphasis off what is really important for stamina, energy and health. What you need is a sensible eating, exercise and energy plan such as the one I am proposing. Some executives have the mistaken notion that they can eat and drink whatever they like, smoke and drink to excess and work themselves to the bone with no ill effects as long as they are taking their 20 vitamin pills every day. This is pure nonsense and, believe me, this is the wrong way to go. I can promise you more energy and stamina than you could get from 1000 vitamin pills.

You should be particularly concerned *if you are taking megadoses of vitamin A, vitamin C, niacin, vitamin B$_6$ (pyridoxine), vitamin D or the mineral selenium.* (What constitutes a megadose for each of these is outlined next.) If you are taking megadoses of any of these to give you more energy, forget it. They actually may be robbing your body of stamina and may be having detrimental effects on your health.

Overdoses of these vitamins and minerals can have the following negative influences on you:

Vitamin A

Vitamin A aids in the formation and maintenance of the skin and the mucous membranes lining the intestines. It is also very important to our vision, since it promotes adaptation to dim light. Deficiencies in vitamin A cause a weakening of body tissues, lowered resistance to infection, stunted growth in children and a lack of ability to see in dim light (sometimes referred to as night blindness).

The recommended daily allowance of Vitamin A for women is 4000 IU (International Units) and for men is 5000 IU. Vitamin A is found in liver, eggs, cheese, butter, yellow vegetables, cantaloupe, carrots, apricots, sweet potatoes, green leafy vegetables and fish liver oil. (Although eggs, cheese and butter are good sources of vitamin A, you should be aware that they are high in fat.)

Continued doses of vitamin A beyond 10 to 15 times the recommended daily allowance can be toxic. Symptoms of overdose are excessive irritability, restlessness, hair loss, muscle pains, headaches, swelling over the long bones, generalized weakness and decalcification of bones. A great excess of vitamin A over a prolonged period of time can result in death.

Vitamin C

You need only 60 mg of vitamin C each day. Vitamin C is found in citrus fruits (especially oranges and grapefruit), tomatoes, potatoes, strawberries, cantaloupe, green peppers and cabbage. These foods contain between 20 mg and 60 mg per individual portion, with citrus fruits being the highest. Megadoses of 1500 mg or more daily can interfere with the absorption of copper in your intestinal tract. Since copper helps to release iron from storage and is vital to the formation of iron-containing protein in red blood cells, iron deficiency anemia may result from megadoses. One of the prime symptoms of anemia is fatigue and lack of stamina. Many executives take vitamin C supplements to ward off colds or possibly because, if they smoke, they have heard that smokers need more vitamin C. Although heavy smokers may need about 25% more vitamin C, you don't need more than 60 mg per day no matter what the situation. The relationship between cold prevention and vitamin C megadoses is not supported by any reputable study and it certainly isn't worth risking anemia.

Niacin

Niacin is classed as a B vitamin. It has been mistakenly referred to in health food literature as vitamin B_3, although there is no historic basis for this reference. Although pantothenic acid (another B vitamin) was often called vitamin B_3 (since it was the third B vitamin to be discovered) in the 1930s, that reference is now obsolete; currently there is no vitamin legitimately known by the name vitamin B_3.

Niacin is essential for growth and health of tissue; it fosters normal appetite and digestion. It also promotes healthy skin and nerves. Lack of niacin results in a disorder known as *pellagra*, characterized by a red rash on the face and hands, mental confusion, irritability and diarrhea.

The recommended daily allowance of niacin for women is 13 mg per day and for men 18 mg per day. Niacin is found in whole grains, fish, poultry, lima beans, soybeans, sesame seeds and brown rice.

Overdoses of niacin (two to three grams or more per day) can result in dilation of the blood vessels and a red rash on the skin.

Vitamin B_6

You need only two mg of vitamin B_6 or pyridoxine per day. Vitamin B_6 is needed by the body for protein metabolism and is found in such foods as fish, pork, whole-grain cereals, nuts and seeds, beans, whole wheat breads, bananas, poultry and raisins. These foods contain between .30 and .90 mg per individual serving, with fish and chicken being in the high end of the range. Many women executives believe that megadoses of this vitamin may help to alleviate premenstrual syndrome, excessive water retention and depression. The side effects of doses of vitamin B_6 over 200 mg per day can be *devastating*. These doses have resulted in a nervous system dysfunction which causes numbness in the feet and hands, and impairment in the sensations of touch and temperature. This side effect can become so pronounced that the victim appears crippled. Luckily, once you stop taking your daily vitamin overdose the symptoms begin to clear up.

Vitamin D

The recommended dosage of vitamin D is only 400 I.U. per day. Vitamin D is used by your body for proper bone calcification; in fact, this vitamin is especially important for women because it helps your body utilize calcium. Doses several hundred times in excess of the daily requirement can result in calcium deposits in your kidneys, blood vessels, heart and lungs.

The best way to get your daily dose of vitamin D is through milk, fish and sunlight. In fact, five minutes in the sun each day (provided you expose more skin than simply your face and hands) fulfills your daily vitamin D requirement.

Selenium

A safe dose of the mineral selenium is about 50 to 200 ug (micrograms) per day. Selenium occurs naturally in all seafood, meat and grains. It would be extremely difficult to have problems meeting your daily requirement even if you were eating a marginal diet. Doses higher than 5000 micrograms per day can result in extreme fatigue, stomach upsets, hair loss and skin discoloration. Recently, the Federal Drug Administration (FDA) took a commercially sold selenium tablet off the market after several cases of vitamin toxicity were reported. These tablets contained 25,000 to 30,000 ug of selenium each. The possible liver damage resulting from just four of these pills taken together could have been fatal.

If you are taking vitamin or mineral megadoses, I suggest you stop immediately. These overdoses do not provide you with one ounce more stamina, and, as I have shown, they may actually rob you of the energy you need in the business world.

If you are not suffering from any illness or deficiency and follow the Hilton Head plan, you will not need megadoses of vitamin or mineral supplements. The one exception is during the time you are on my weight loss plan, when you should take a multivitamin with a mineral supplement. This is just insurance against deficiency since your food intake on the weight loss plan is lower than normal. If you wish to take a multivitamin with a mineral supplement all the time, even on my maintenance plans, feel free to do so. The dosages in a multivitamin certainly won't hurt you as long as no megadoses of any vitamin or mineral appear on the label. Consult your physician about which multivitamin and mineral supplement you should take.

Since women have special vitamin/mineral needs please refer to Chapter 16 for more details on my guidelines for women executives.

10

▼

The Hilton Head Lifetime Stamina Fitness Plan

There is no getting around the fact that as an executive you spend a great deal of your time in a sitting position. The management responsibilities you have, for the most part, require the use of your brain—not your body. Too much high-level mental activity without at least some physical activity to balance you out results in fatigue and less than desirable performance levels.

A sedentary lifestyle deconditions the body in such a way that you're functioning at only half your normal energy potential. Many times you're not even aware that you're getting weaker and weaker by not using your body.

Four Reasons Why You Need This Fitness Plan

This fitness plan is an absolute must if you are serious about your career in management. While you certainly will be able to increase your energy level to some degree without the exercise component of my program, you will never be able to reach your physical and mental prime.

As an executive you need my stamina fitness plan for four reasons:

REASON NUMBER 1: The stamina fitness plan will give you a reserve of energy and stamina.

Since the business world is so unpredictable, a reserve of strength and stamina is essential in your life. You must be ready to summon inner strength at a moment's notice.

It has been proven again and again that regular, moderate physical activity of the type I advise builds up a reserve of strength and energy in your body. One of the first things managers who come to me for help experience after only a few days on my exercise plan is a tremendous surge of energy. Their muscles feel stronger, they can breathe more easily, and they can last longer doing just about anything.

An international banker who had been following my exercise plan for three months related this story:

> "Your fitness plan has made me a new person. I'm not exactly Superwoman, but you'd think so if you saw me in action. Last week I got the flu a day before I had to travel to Zurich to present a major address to a conference of bank managers from around the world. Because I was involved in two major oil financing deals before I left New York, I had gone for two nights with very little sleep. Thank goodness for the reserves of energy I had been building up through your fitness plan. Not only did I close the two deals successfully but, in spite of the flu, I flew to Switzerland and gave the best presentation of my life. I know I never could have done it three months ago."

There is a real *physiological reason* why my exercise plan will stockpile extra energy for future use. It has to do with your maximum oxygen capacity, or what is sometimes called your maximum oxygen uptake. Your maximum oxygen capacity refers to the total amount of oxygen you utilize from the air you breathe. Executives who follow my recommendations actually draw more oxygen out of the air they breathe than they did before. Once inhaled, this oxygen is used more efficiently than before. The important fact here is that the more oxygen you breathe in from the air, the more energy and stamina you will have.

From a scientific standpoint, your maximum oxygen capacity is equal to the number of milliliters of oxygen that you use from the air each minute per kilogram of body weight. This number can be calculated by means of an oxygen consumption test. You normally would not take such a test unless you were undergoing a very thorough physical fitness evaluation, but you may want to request one as part of your new program of health.

Your level of fatigue at work is directly related to the percentage of your maximum oxygen capacity the work requires. The higher the percentage, the higher your fatigue.

Let's suppose that you have a maximum oxygen capacity of 30; that is, as you breathe, you take in 30 milliliters of oxygen per kilogram of your body weight each minute. A graduate of my Hilton Head executive stamina program might have a maximum oxygen capacity of 45. Both of you weigh the same. Now let's further assume that one afternoon you have to rush home on a moment's notice, pack for a trip to Philadelphia, rush off to the airport, take your flight, arrive 30 minutes late, jump into a taxi and head for a meeting where you are expected to deliver a detailed briefing upon arrival. This rather stressful, "rushing around" behavior might require as much as 20 milliliters of oxygen per body weight per minute, just for you to complete the physical and mental effort involved.

Assuming that your maximum capacity is 30 you would be using two-thirds of your maximum energy just to get through this schedule for the afternoon. My "graduate" with the oxygen capacity of 45 would be working at only 44% of his capacity. To accomplish the same activity, your body would have to work harder and expend more energy than his. Because of this, your mind and body would give out sooner than his.

My executive fitness plan will improve your maximum oxygen capacity so that jobs which now require 50% or 60% of your energy will call for only 30% or 40% in the future. This gives you a 20% to 30% reserve to use for something else!

REASON NUMBER 2: The stamina plan will make you more creative and enable you to make better decisions.

I have had manager after manager tell me how the program has dramatically boosted their clarity of thinking in business.

"I'm definitely more creative," said one account executive. "It sounds funny, but I feel that my mind has more energy, as if my brain has more electrical power. I'm coming up with one new concept or idea right after the other. I feel great about it since I didn't know I had that much creative energy in me. Your program has unlocked my mind and given me a great deal more confidence in myself."

This is not an unusual experience. I hear this kind of enthusiasm over mental improvements all the time.

While my fitness plan cannot make you more intelligent, it can definitely improve your ability to sort through information in your mind and make complex decisions.

With these kinds of results, what are you waiting for?

REASON NUMBER 3: The stamina fitness plan will even out your moods and help you overcome stress.

Emotional stability and stress reduction are two of the most important benefits of my exercise plan for executives. The tension, irritability and emotional ups-and-downs of the business day can exhaust you. It might be a subordinate who does only a so-so job, leaving you to handle your own work and part of his; or it might be a colleague who is trying every political trick in the book to get the promotion that you deserve; or how about the boss who gives you important tasks to perform in the company but not the ultimate decision-making power to follow through with your solutions to problems?

These exercises reduce anxiety and agitation and lead to an enhanced feeling of well-being. I have seen irritable and edgy executives calm down completely in just a few days after beginning this exercise plan. Little day-by-day annoyances at work don't even bother them any more. And they don't take a negative mood home with them, either.

Mild to moderate depression also improves with the Hilton Head lifetime exercise plan. Psychologists and psychiatrists have used physical fitness programs in the treatment of mild depression and found that they can be as effective as more traditional medical treatments.

One reason why exercise alleviates negative emotions is that regular physical activity actually changes body chemistry. Exercise stimulates the brain's production of the hormone norepinephrine. This hormone is related to emotional stability. People with balanced emotions have high levels of norepinephrine while chronically depressed people have very low levels.

Exercise may also stimulate substances in the brain called endorphins. These brain chemicals are referred to as "natural opiates" because they are actually morphine-like substances that our brains produce. Endorphins give us a good feeling or a natural high.

I believe that exercise is like free psychotherapy. It relaxes you, gives you a feeling of peace and helps you control your emotions. What more could you ask?

REASON NUMBER 4: The stamina fitness plan will lower your risk factors associated with cardiovascular disease.

I have consistently found that the exercise plan I prescribe greatly reduces risk factors associated with heart attack and stroke. When practiced together with my nutritional program, it lowers cholesterol, blood pressure and blood sugar level.

While many professionals hedge on the relationship between exercise and cardiovascular health, I am convinced of it. I'm not alone in my convictions. One of the most convincing recent studies of this relationship was reported in the prestigious *Journal of the American Medical Association* (July, 1984) by Dr. Ralph S. Paffenbarger Jr. of Harvard University, a noted authority on heart disease. He analyzed the health histories of over 16,000 Harvard alumni from 1962 to 1978. (You could very well have been one of his subjects if you were a Harvard graduate between the ages of 35 and 78 during the period of his study.)

Dr. Paffenbarger studied over 500 of these alumni who had suffered a first heart attack and survived and over 1400 who had died from coronary heart disease during this time. His research demonstrated conclusively that regular exercise after graduating from college coincided with low coronary heart-disease risk. Those alumni who were sedentary—even if they had been varsity athletes—had a high risk of heart attack and stroke.

With all the publicity about the death of Jim Fixx, author of *The Complete Book of Running*, during his daily run and about others who have suffered heart attacks while exercising, physical fitness has gotten a tarnished *bad* name. No matter what you hear, a daily regimen of moderate exercise *is* good for you: It will give you more stamina and energy and improve your overall health. It will *not* make you immortal. Obviously, if you have a history of heart disease in your family, high blood pressure and obesity, you have a greater risk of heart attack than someone without these factors. If you were to die of a heart attack while exercising should the conclusion be that exercise is bad for people? Of course not! What if you were to die while participating in a heated political debate? Would we conclude that politics is fatal? Perhaps, on that issue, there would be some debate!

There is one other factor about exercise that is quite important. If you have a weight problem draining your energy, the stamina fitness plan is a must. Not only will you be burning calories, but you'll be stimulating your metabolism to burn calories *faster* even when you are not exercising. My executives who exercise as I advise have a higher basal metabolism even when they are sitting behind their desks than their sedentary colleagues. Regular exercise stimulates your body to burn more calories throughout the day even when you are resting.

My 4/3 Weekly Exercise Routine

The first thing I want you to know about this fitness program is that it is designed for your busy lifestyle. I'm not trying to turn you into a fitness fanatic or train you for the next Olympic Games. I realize that your time is limited and that time is money.

To set you straight right off the bat, my exercise program:

- Is easy to follow.
- Does not require you to be an athlete.
- Is designed for the average person.
- Does not require you to jog or run
  (unless you choose to).

Moreover, the plan requires you to spend only 20 to 40 minutes every day. I call it a 4/3 plan because it's divided into four days of *stamina striding* and three days of *stamina strengthening* exercises. The secret is consistency, not intensity. I want you doing moderate exercise every day rather than intense exercise on weekends. There's a classic question in the field of preventive medicine that, sadly, might currently apply to you. The query is "When does the weekend athlete die?" The answer, of course, is "On the weekend." I would rather you not exercise at all than play several strenuous sets of tennis on the weekend but do nothing all week long. Remember, you shouldn't play sports occasionally to get in shape but you should get in shape to play sports!

Your Doctor's Advice

Even though this is a moderate exercise program, you should *consult your physician before starting it*. Show him my plan and discuss it. Physicians should certainly approve of my system and would probably encourage you to get started as quickly as possible. Your physician may wish, however, to put you through a medical examination including a stress test, or treadmill electrocardiogram, especially if you are over 40 years of age or have any significant risk factors for cardiovascular disease.

The Stamina Stride

My fitness program is based on what I have termed the *stamina stride*: a brisk walk designed to increase your maximum oxygen capacity and build up energy reserves.

This exercise consists of three basic components:

1. The warm-up phase
2. The stamina-stride phase
3. The cool-down phase

Warm-Up Phase

To get your body ready for the Stamina Stride and to prevent soreness afterwards, you should spend five minutes before the stride going through the following warm-up routine. The warm-up routine gets the blood flowing to your muscles to ready them for the stamina stride. Contrary to popular belief, *you should not stretch your muscles prior to a walk or run*. Stretching "cold" muscles does little to increase flexibility. Your warm-up routine should be designed to gently move and flex muscles but not to *stretch* them; the best time to stretch your muscles to increase their flexibility is *after* walking or running. This is common knowledge among exercise physiologists but most people stretch before they walk or run and then fail to stretch afterward when it would do them the most good. Stretching beforehand is a waste of time.

These four warm-up exercises should be done prior to your stamina stride:

ROPE CLIMB

The rope climb flexes the muscles in your sides and shoulders.

- Stand straight with arms at sides. Reach one arm into the air as if stretching up to the sky.

- Bring that arm down slowly and reach up with the other arm.

- Your motion should be smooth and gentle as if slowly climbing an imaginary rope.

- Continue for about one minute.

Figure 10-1 Rope Climb

SHOULDER SHRUG

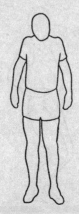

Figure 10-2 Shoulder Shrug

The shoulder shrug loosens the muscles in your shoulders, upper back and neck.

- Stand straight with arm at sides. Bring shoulders straight up as if trying to touch them to your ears.

- As soon as you feel a tightening in the shoulder muscles, bring shoulders back down again.

- Continue for 10 repetitions in a slow, steady manner.

HALF-SQUATS

Half-squats are designed to get the blood flowing to the muscles in your legs. If you have any problems with your knees, skip this exercise and go on to the next one.

- Stand straight, placing hands on hips. Bend knees about halfway and sink into a half squat.

Figure 10-3 Half-Squats

- *Do not bend all the way down*. Keep back straight and heels flat on the floor.

- Straighten legs and stand erect. Do about 1 squat (down and up) every 2 to 3 seconds until you complete 10 to 15 squats. Movements should be slow and smooth.

- If you feel unsteady, rest hands on the back of a chair as you do your half-squats.

ABDOMINAL CURLS

An abdominal curl is like a sit-up, except that it puts more stress on your stomach muscles and less on your back. Your stomach muscles must do all the work.

- Lie on back with legs bent at the knees and feet flat on the floor. *Never do this exercise with legs straight out*.

- Fold hands across chest. Now curl your body up slowly to a 30° angle, starting by moving head forward and then bringing the rest of your body up, vertebra by vertebra.

- Come back down slowly, vertebra by vertebra. Rhythm should be smooth and slow. Unlike a sit-up, you do not want to bring your body all the way up to a sitting position.

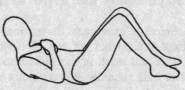

Figure 10-4 Abdominal Curls

- Try to do 10 to 15 repetitions at a slow, easy pace. If this is too much at first, start off with 5 or 6 and gradually work your way up to 15 over 2 to 3 weeks.

The Stamina-Stride Phase

After five minutes of warming up you are ready for the stamina stride. This brisk walk should be the mainstay of your fitness program. It will give you as much energy as you need for your business day. You do not have to run, do aerobic dance or work out at a health club, unless you want to. You may already be jogging or enrolled in a fitness class. If what you are doing is compatible with my recommendations, by all means, continue if you enjoy it and are doing it without strain.

Let's examine some of the components of the stamina stride:

What Kind of a Walk Is the Stamina Stride?

The stamina stride is a moderate paced, relaxed walk. The intensity will be determined by your fitness level to begin with. (I'll explain how to determine your speed in just a minute.) Many of my clients end up walking at about a 15 minute per mile pace. You may need to start out at a 30 minute per mile pace, however, and work up to a faster walk. This is particularly true if you are sedentary or overweight.

Just keep a nice, relaxed pace. Swing your arms freely. Keep your back straight but not stiff. Do not take overly long strides. This will result in shin splints and lower back discomfort. Just walk naturally. Be careful not to slump over as you walk.

I suggest to all of my clients that they purchase a good pair of running shoes for walking. These shoes are specifically designed to hold your foot steady and cushion your heel as you walk. If you go to a reputable sporting goods or running store, the salesperson should be able to recommend the type of running shoe that best suits your needs. If you have flat feet or an extremely high arch you may want to consult a podiatrist who might suggest a certain shoe or a special insert. He can also help you if you have a tendency to toe-in or toe-out as you walk.

Make sure your walk is continuous and nonstop. This means no window shopping or stopping to talk with friends. Where I live on Hilton Head that means no stopping along the beach for seashells!

How Often Should You Walk?

To gain the stamina you need you must walk four days each week. Any four days will do, but it's a good idea to walk every other day during the week. If you want to walk more frequently, be my guest! That's perfectly okay. You must walk four days a week, however, to have an impact on your stamina level.

How Long Should You Walk?

You must walk for at least 30 minutes to increase your energy level. Again, if you want to walk for a longer period of time, that's fine. Many of my clients find that once they get started they keep going for 45 to 60 minutes. Just remember that 30 minutes is the minimum.

How Fast Should You Walk?

The intensity of your walk is determined by your initial fitness level. If you walk too slowly, you may not increase your stamina at all. If you walk too quickly you may tire yourself out before you finish your 30 minutes. Also, you may be pushing too hard too soon and end up hurting yourself.

As part of your initial warm-up it is very important that you walk very slowly for the first five minutes to warm and limber up your muscles. This will help prevent injury to your muscles.

There are two ways to find out how intensely you should walk for the remainder of your stamina stride. The first method is the easiest and the one I recommend the most. It is called the perceived exertion test. This is a very simple, subjective rating scale of the amount of effort you are using during your walk. Soon after you begin the stamina stride, ask yourself "How much effort is involved in the current pace of my walk?" Give your answer in terms of one of the following seven categories:

1. Very, very light
2. Very light
3. Fairly light
4. Somewhat hard
5. Hard
6. Very hard
7. Very, very hard

You will be increasing your reserve of stamina if your effort is in the "somewhat hard" to "hard" categories. If you feel you are in categories 6 or 7, slow down; you are walking much too fast for your level of fitness. If you are in categories 1, 2 or 3, speed up a bit; you are not pushing yourself hard enough.

This perceived exertion test may not sound very scientific, but I assure you it is. Subjective ratings using this system correspond extremely well to actual measures of heart rate and oxygen capacity. Once you use this test a few times, you'll know just how fast you should walk to increase your stamina. As you get in better shape you may have to walk a little faster and the perceived exertion test will allow you to judge just how much faster.

If you score above 5 on this test, you probably won't be able to carry on a normal conversation while walking. You would probably be out of breath. Whenever you feel you would be unable to converse with someone during your walk, *slow down*.

If you want to be more precise about figuring out just how fast you should be walking, you'll have to do some simple calculations. Subtract your age from 220. The resulting number is your theoretical maximum exercise heart rate. To increase your stamina, you should walk at an intensity between 70% and 80% of this maximum. So now figure 70% and then 80% of your maximum heart rate.

Let's suppose you are 40 years old. If we subtract 40 from 220 we get 180. So now we know that your maximum exercise heart rate is 180. With a little more figuring we find that 70% of 180 is 126 and 80% of 180 is 144. Now divide the 70% and 80% figures by 6. In the example I just gave the resulting numbers would be 21 and 24.

These numbers represent your target heart-rate range based on a 10-second pulse reading. The target heart rate range is the rate at which your heart should beat during periods of aerobic exercise in order to increase your stamina level. It is also a range that is safe for you. The best way to take your exercise pulse is to place three fingers on the side of your neck, just between your jawbone and to one side of your Adam's apple. By *gently* pressing in at this point you will feel your pulse beating in the carotid artery. Using the second hand on your watch, count the number of pulse beats in 10 seconds while you are walking. In the example I cited, if the executive's 10-second pulse was between 21 and 24 beats, then he or she would be walking at just the right pace to derive cardiovascular benefit from the walk.

Although it can't hurt to know your target range, I find the perceived exertion method a lot simpler and more in line with how much effort you're really expending.

When Should You Walk?

Once your day begins in the world of management, your life is only partially your own. This is why it's best to get your stamina stride in early, first thing in the morning. With business lunches and meetings often lasting longer than expected, it is very difficult to have time for a warm-up, stamina walk and cool-down in the middle of the day. If you're like most executives, you may not be certain when your business day is going to end. Unless you are very much in control of your own schedule and unless you arrive home at about the same time every evening, you're better off walking in the morning before your work day begins.

Since you are doing your stamina walks only four days a week, two of those days could be on the weekends. This would be especially practical if you have a long commute into work and have to wake up very early just to get there on time.

If you arrive at home at a reasonable hour at least two or three evenings a week, you might prefer to do your walking then. This strategy can help you unwind and can serve as a buffer zone between the business world and your family and social life. It may also eliminate your taste for a cocktail to help you unwind and make the transition from workday to home and hearth.

How to Fit Exercise into a Busy Schedule

1. Remind yourself that time for your health and stamina is as important as anything or anyone else in your daily schedule.

2. Inform family, friends and co-workers about your exercise time and let them know you are unavailable during that time.

3. Don't allow others to demean your exercise efforts or make you feel as if you were wasting time or indulging yourself when you should be working.

4. Delegate authority and ask others to help you make time for exercise.

5. If you view exercise as a time robber, remember that *because* of exercise you will feel more energetic and able to accomplish more in less time.

What About Bad Weather?

Unless it's a real downpour with gusts of wind, I suggest you take your scheduled walk whether it's raining or not. Just dress appropriately. In heavy rain, snow, ice or extreme cold you certainly could choose another day or have an indoor exercise alternative handy. For example, I recommend to most of my executives that they purchase a treadmill or exercycle for inclement weather. People who are in the habit of walking enjoy a treadmill as an indoor alternative more than the exercise bicycle.

Is Walking All You Need for Complete Stamina?

You may be skeptical about walking being enough to keep you healthy and energetic. Well, my stamina walk *is* enough if you are walking briskly enough to reach my "somewhat hard" and "hard" categories of perceived exertion. You may find that after you get more physically fit, the walking becomes easier and you can pick up your pace. You may even find that you become so accustomed to very brisk walking that it no longer is as strenuous as it should be.

If this happens you will need to increase your effort by carrying hand-held weights, which are discussed in more detail in the next section. Any lightweight dumbbells will do. There are more elaborate hand weights on the market, known as HeavyHands™, that have handles, making them very easy to carry with you on your walk. Weights that weigh about two pounds each for women and two to three pounds each for men should be sufficient to increase your effort to the desired level. Wearing a small knapsack weighted with books would accomplish the same thing as hand weights.

The Cool-Down Phase

Now that your muscles are warmed up, stretching will have a tremendous influence on your overall flexibility. Flexibility is an important factor in your overall fitness as an executive. If you are flexible, you won't tire as easily when you are forced to sit in one position for hours at a time. These four flexibility stretches should be done after your stamina stride.

WALL STRETCH

This exercise stretches out your calf muscles and the Achilles tendon, which is located just above your heel.

- Stand about 12 inches from a wall or tree. Move one leg straight behind so it is about 12 to 15 inches behind your other leg. Lean toward the wall, placing palms flat on its surface.

- Keep arms straight, but bend front leg slightly at the knee. *Keep the back leg straight* and the heel flat on the floor. Lean in gently, feeling the stretch in the Achilles tendon. Hold that position for 15 seconds. If this maneuver is painful you are stretching too far. Ease up a bit.

- Now stretch a little more and hold it for 30 seconds. Do the same stretch with the other leg. *Do not bounce.* Do this and all the other stretches only once.

Figure 10-5 Wall Stretch

SIT AND REACH

This exercise stretches the muscles in your lower back and hamstring area (the back part of your thigh).

Figure 10-6 Sit and Reach

- If you have a history of back problems especially in the lower part of your back, do this and the next stretch very, very gently. *If you have current back problems, consult your physician before doing any of these stretches*.

- Sit on the floor with legs extended in front and feet together. Bend forward slowly, curling your back as you go. Reach outstretched arms toward toes and head toward knees.

- You are not actually trying to touch your toes. Do not risk a pulled muscle. Be gentle and never bounce as you stretch. Hold stretch for 15 seconds. Then stretch a little farther and hold for 30 seconds.

INNER THIGH STRETCH

This stretch is designed for your inner thigh and groin muscles.

- Sit on the floor with knees bent to the sides and the soles of feet together. Hold onto toes. Keep elbows on

Figure 10-7 Inner Thigh Stretch

the outside of legs. pull forward very gently, bending from hips.

- When inner thigh muscles are stretching, hold that position for 15 seconds. Then bend a little further and hold for another 30 seconds. Sit up straight and relax.

BACK ROLLER

This is a good overall relaxing stretch, which increases flexibility in your lower back.

- Lie on your back on the floor. Bend one leg up toward you, holding onto bent knee as you bring it close into your body. (Lower back should stay pressed against the floor.)

- Hold bent leg for 30 seconds and then let it come back down to the floor. Repeat with the other leg. Now bring both knees toward chest and hold for another 30 seconds.

Figure 10-8 Back Roller

My Eight Stamina Strengtheners

The stamina walk will increase your body's energy reserve and intensify your heart and lung capacity. From a muscular point of view, walking has more of a strengthening effect on the muscles in the lower part of your body. To give you *total* stamina, you must also spend a little time on developing upper body strength. Otherwise, your upper body muscles will tire easily from inactivity and static tension at work.

On the three days during the week that you are not doing the stamina walk, you should schedule my stamina strengtheners. These stamina strengtheners require only 20 minutes of your time.

To do the stamina strengtheners, you'll need a pair of hand-held weights. You can purchase these from any local sporting-goods store. Any style will do. The least expensive hand-held weights are made either of iron or of plastic filled with sand. There's even a plastic variety that you fill with water to provide the weight. These are ideal for traveling, since you can just add the water weight at your destination.

Women usually start out by using three to five pound weights while men can often handle six to eight pounds. You want weights that you can handle easily. You don't need to buy the type that weight lifters use. Just buy the simplest ones you can find to start out with.

Choose a weight that is light enough to enable you to lift it with one arm about 10 times without overly fatiguing yourself. The HeavyHands™ weights I mentioned before are also quite good since you can change the weight very easily by unscrewing the ends and adding different poundage.

As you practice these exercises, remember that you are not trying to lift a lot of heavy weight. For the kind of stamina and firmness we are after it is better to lift light weights with many repetitions than heavy weights only a few times. The former builds stamina; the latter builds bulk.

Three days a week, preferably with at least one day's rest in between, do the following eight stamina strengtheners:

CURL

The curl strengthens and firms the front part of your upper arm (the bicep).

- Stand straight with arms at sides, holding one weight in each hand. Palm should be facing forward.

- Bending arm at the elbow, lift the elbow and lift the weight up to shoulder. Then slowly bring it back down.

- Repeat 12 to 15 times. Rest briefly and do 12 to 15 more repetitions with the same arm. Now repeat with the other arm.

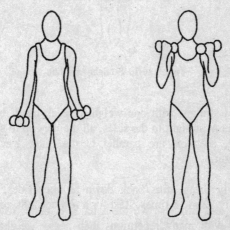

Figure 10-9 Curl

- If unable to lift the weight 12 to 15 times the weight you are using is too heavy for you. Use a lighter weight to begin with.

STRAIGHT-ARM LIFT

This lift strengthens and firms the muscles in the shoulders and the upper arms.

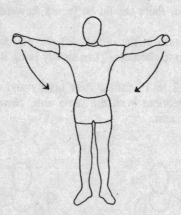

Figure 10-10 Straight-Arm Lift

- Stand straight with one weight in each hand. Now lift arms out straight to the sides, all the way up to shoulder level, so arms are parallel to the floor. Keep arms straight.

- Slowly bring arms back down to your sides. Repeat slowly 12 to 15 times. Rest for a few seconds and do 12 to 15 more repetitions.

SIDE BENDS

The side bends are great exercises for your waist and sides.

Figure 10-11 Side Bends

- With arm bent at the elbow, hold one weight on shoulder. Other arm should be straight down at your side with the weight in your hand.

- Bend sideways toward straight-arm side until you feel the muscles along the other side of your body stretching out. Straighten, repeat 12 to 15 times, rest and repeat again.

- Switch positions and repeat two sets of 12 to 15 repetitions each on the other side.

MILITARY PRESS

This is especially good for your shoulders and the backs of your arm.

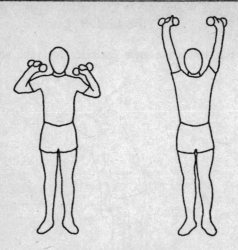

Figure 10-12 Military Press

- With arms bent at the elbows, hold the weights on shoulders. Push both weights straight up until arms are perfectly straight over your head.

- Now bring weights down to shoulders in a slow, fluid motion. Repeat 12 to 15 times, rest and repeat 12 to 15 more times.

TRICEP EXTENSION

This exercise is great for the back part of your upper arm, an area that is usually flabby because of very little use.

- Hold only one weight. Start with arms straight down, palms facing outward. Then raise your hand and arm with the weight straight up from your shoulder over your head.

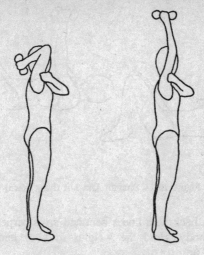

Figure 10-13 Tricep Extension

- Bending your arm at the elbow, let the weight fall slowly backward toward the upper part of your back. With your other hand, grab hold of your elbow, keeping it from moving.

- Now lift the weight back up, so your arm is fully extended over your head again. Again let the weight fall backward and grip your bent elbow. Keep your elbow steady and facing forward.

- Repeat 12 to 15 times, rest and repeat 12 to 15 times again. Switch weight to the other hand and repeat.

STRAIGHT-ARM LIFT (LYING DOWN)

This exercise works on the muscles in your chest and upper arms.

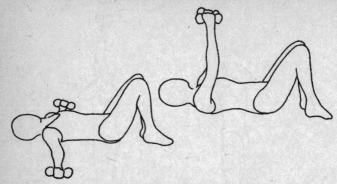

Figure 10-14 Straight-Arm Lift (lying down)

- Lie on back with knees bent and arms perpendicular to your body. Hold the weights in your hands, palms facing up.

- Bend arms *slightly* at the elbows, and smoothly lift the weights above your body so that hands come in contact with one another. Keep lower back pressed to the floor.

- Slowly bring arms back down to the floor. Repeat 12 to 15 repetitions 2 times.

- Keep knees bent as you do this exercise. This presses the lower back to the floor, strengthening the abdominal muscles.

BENCH PRESS

The bench press firms your chest and the back of your upper arms.

- Lie flat on your back on the floor, knees bent, arms perpendicular to body, holding a weight in each hand. Bend elbows so that they rest on the floor by your sides

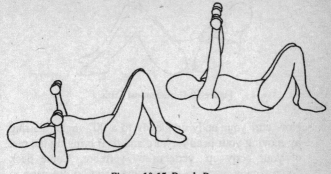

Figure 10-15 Bench Press

and you are holding the weights up in the air. Your palm should be facing outward toward your toes.

- Push both arms up simultaneously so that arms are straight and fully extended upward. Do not let the lower back arch off the floor during the extension.

- Slowly bring arms down, resting elbows on the floor once again. Repeat 12 to 15 times, in a slow fluid motion. Rest and repeat 12 to 15 times.

ABDOMINAL CURLS

For this last stamina strengthener, you won't need the hand weights. This exercise is specifically for your stomach muscles. An abdominal curl is like a sit-up, but the curl strengthens your stomach muscles without straining your lower back.

- Lie on your back with knees bent and feet flat on the floor. *Never do this exercise with legs straight out*. Fold hands across chest.

Figure 10-16 Abdominal Curls

- Now curl your body up slowly to a 30° angle, starting by moving your head forward and then bringing the rest of your body up, vertebra by vertebra. Come back down slowly, vertebra by vertebra. You do not need to sit up all the way.

- Repeat 10 times, rest and repeat 10 more times. Over a few weeks work up to 20 repetitions repeated 3 times. After this becomes easy, you can increase resistance by holding a weight (perhaps 2 pounds to begin with) against your chest as you curl up. As you become stronger you can increase resistance by gradually increasing the size of the weights.

A Final Word About the Stamina Strengtheners

Make sure you breathe normally while you are doing the stamina strengtheners. You may have a tendency to hold your breath as you lift the weights. This is not a good practice. You should breathe normally as you do these exercises and avoid the tendency to hold your breath.

These strengtheners should be done slowly and easily. Don't rush through them.

My 10 Exercise Motivators

To gain maximum stamina and energy, you should take your stamina walk four times each week and do the stamina strengtheners on the other three days. I realize, however, that because you are human you may have some days that you just don't feel like exercising, even though my Hilton Head plan takes very little effort.

My main advice to you is to schedule your exercise at about the same time every day. This regularity will help to establish exercise as a habit. Then you'll be able to stop thinking about it—you'll walk simply because it's time to walk.

I remember asking a woman attorney who had been through my program about seven years ago why she walked every morning from 6:30 a.m. to 7:15 a.m. Her reply was astonishingly simple, "Because that's what I do at 6:30 every morning." No other reason was necessary. She had established such a strong habit that she didn't have to convince herself every morning that exercise was good for her. She just did it. It is ingrained like brushing your teeth every day. If I came into your house first thing in the morning and asked why you were brushing your teeth, you wouldn't give me a long discourse on oral hygiene. You'd probably tell me the same thing my client did. You'd say, "Because that's what I do soon after I get up every day." Strong habits need no explanation.

On those days when you don't feel like exercising, here are 10 ways to motivate yourself:

1. Try the *one-minute principle*. Put on your exercise clothes and shoes, go outside for your stamina stride and walk for one minute. Chances are, once you're outside you'll keep on going. The first step is always the most difficult.

2. Make a list of the most important long-term benefits of exercise. Close your eyes and imagine yourself after a year of regular exercise, experiencing more energy and stamina than you've ever had before and looking great, too!

3. Promise yourself a special treat (preferably non-edible) if you do your exercise.

4. Visualize yourself being physically active and really enjoying it. Conjure up feelings of being super-energized and totally in control of your body.

5. Think of yourself as a good example of fitness and health for a close friend, relative or co-worker who should be exercising but isn't.

6. Write down your excuses for not wanting to exercise or, better yet, dictate them into a tape recorder and play them back. As you listen, argue with what you hear, as if you were your own best friend.

7. Turn exercise into a fantasy game. Pretend your exercise session is the Olympics and the whole world is watching. Over 200 million Americans are counting on you to get out there and give it all you've got for the gold.

8. Make sure you are considering exercise as a choice and not a duty. If you say, "I choose to walk" rather than "I *have* to walk" you are less likely to rebel.

9. Add music to your exercise routine. Try a stereo headset with your favorite music.

10. Avoid "all-or-nothing" thinking. If you don't feel like exercising as much as usual, plan a shorter routine. *Some* exercise is better than none.

11

▼

Twenty Minutes to Greater Stamina

In addition to the basic stamina lifetime routine of high-energy eating and exercise you can also use the *resting-in-motion routine* to give you super stamina above and beyond your new baseline energy level. In just twenty short minutes, this routine attacks the executive fatigue factors at their roots so that you are not just pepping yourself up temporarily, but are actually *eradicating* the major causes of your lack of stamina for the rest of the day.

The routine should be scheduled three times per week. On those days when you completely run out of time, due to travel or marathon meetings, you can substitute the Three-Minute booster routine that is described in the next chapter. The resting-in-motion routine is particularly helpful on very hectic, enervating days. I suggest you schedule time for the routine either in the mid-morning or in mid to late afternoon.

Remember, *repetition is the key*. After repeated sessions, your body and mind will become conditioned to reaching superior levels of energy and stamina.

Once you realize that this routine is a necessity for full-throttle stamina, committing your time for it is essential for the full program to work for you. When I discuss time commitments I often think of Roger, the 38-year-old president of a wholesale food distributorship. When he first came to me, he was overweight, under enormous business stress and on the brink of a marital break-up. His blood pressure and cholesterol were high and his physician considered him a prime target for a heart attack or stroke.

As you might expect, even though Roger was a business success, he was mildly depressed, fearful about his medical condition and felt like he was losing control of his life. He was especially frustrated because he always took pride in the fact that he was a fiercely independent individual, in charge of his own destiny.

Although his business was doing well, he just didn't have the drive he used to have. He was letting certain responsibilities go and not paying close enough attention to the managers in his distribution centers. Moreover, Roger had made several poor judgments lately about business expansion that had cost him plenty.

He described his feelings in this way:

> "I feel like I'm in a small boat on a choppy sea,
> without oars. I'm being bounced here and there.
> And what's worse, I don't have the energy and
> drive to do anything about it."

I started him on my basic stamina nutrition and fitness plans and taught him the 20-minute resting-in-motion routine. He followed my advice to the letter and after several weeks he felt a charge of energy he had not experienced in years. Work no longer seemed like drudgery; he was stimulated and motivated again. He set new goals and experienced a real joy for life. His employees responded by being more productive. His wife reacted by telephoning me to give thanks that her husband was back to his old self. He was much less moody and preoccupied. He seemed genuinely excited by his work. In fact, within 12 months his company became the number one wholesaler in the midwestern region.

Five years later, Roger got in touch with me to tell me that his stamina had continued. He had lost 40 pounds, his marriage had never been better and his company had hit a new high in profits for the last fiscal year.

What struck me most about Roger was his tenacity in scheduling his resting-in-motion break every day. He was so sold on the rewards of this approach that he was determined not to let anyone or anything get in his way.

He described the Hilton Head program as his "lifeline" to greater and greater levels of energy and success.

The Resting-in-Motion Routine

This routine is divided into five short phases, each to be completed in exactly the same order every time. Schedule twenty minutes three times a week for this routine. Close your office door and make sure you are not disturbed. If you are out of town or not in your office, go back to your hotel room or find an empty meeting room you can use. While doing the entire routine is important, keep in mind that *some* resting-in-motion is better than none.

The five phases of the resting-in-motion routine are

1. Breath of fresh air
2. Stamina Stretch
3. Energy-in-motion
4. Brain booster
5. Power snack

PHASE 1: BREATH OF FRESH AIR

Time to complete: Three minutes

Purpose: To ensure that enough fresh air is reaching your lungs to oxygenate the blood going to your muscles and brain.

Description:

- Take off suit jacket.
- Stand up straight with arms at sides. Breathe in as much air as possible through your nose, trying to fill the lower part of lungs first. Avoid the tendency to pull the stomach in as you breathe.
- Next, fill the middle part of lungs. Finally, continue to inhale while shrugging shoulders and raising them toward the ears. This fills the top part of the lungs with air.
- Hold breath for two to three seconds. Then begin to exhale, forcing air out gradually through nose and mouth. Pull abdomen in and up to release air. Slowly bring shoulders back down as you exhale.
- Repeat, taking slow, deep breaths. Breathe slowly, with each inhale–exhale sequence lasting about 10–15 seconds. Continue these deep breathing sequences for 1½ minutes more.
- Return to normal breathing. Stand up straight with arms at sides.
- Inhale deeply through nose once again. Fill lungs from the bottom up. As you inhale, raise arms straight out from sides in a smooth motion and extend up in the air above your head. Hold the breath for two to three seconds.
- Now exhale slowly through your nose. As you exhale,

lower arms back down to sides. Repeat these deep breathing sequences for one minute; rest. Repeat again for 30 seconds. Breathe slowly and smoothly. If you feel a little dizzy or light-headed, you are breathing too quickly or too deeply.

Review:

1. Stand with arms at sides.
2. Inhale deeply through nose.
3. Fill lungs from the bottom up, raising shoulders as you inhale.
4. Hold breath for two to three seconds.
5. Exhale slowly through nose and slowly lower shoulders.
6. Continue for 1½ minutes.
7. Repeat the procedure for one minute, raising arms out to sides. Rest, then do this for 30 more seconds.

PHASE 2: STAMINA STRETCH

Time to complete: Four minutes

Purpose: To stretch tension from muscles and lessen feeling of fatigue.

Description:

As you read the descriptions of each exercise refer to the illustration of each.

The first stretch, known as the *rope climb*, requires you to reach and stretch your arms over your head and pretend you are climbing up a rope hanging from the ceiling.

• Alternately stretch up with one arm at a time. Movement

Figure 11–1   Rope Climb

should be slow and gentle, with emphasis on stretching arms, shoulders and chest muscles.
• Continue for about 40 seconds.

Next begin the *reach for the stars*.

• Raise both arms high above head, reaching as far as you can, until you feel your whole body stretching out.
• Continue for 10 seconds; bring arms back down and shake them out. Rest for five seconds.
• Repeat this sequence three times.

Since a great deal of tension can build up in the shoulders, neck and facial muscles, these next few stretches are very important for eliminating fatigue.

Figure 11–2   Reach for the Stars

First comes the *shoulder stretch*.

- Shrug shoulders just as you did during the deep breathing routine. Concentrate on tightening shoulder- and upper-back muscles.
- Hold for ten seconds, then slowly let shoulders drop back down. Repeat four times.

Now for the *Neck Stretch*.
Note: Do this stretch gently so you don't risk a pulled muscle.

- Stand or sit erect, looking straight ahead. Slowly turn head to one side as if looking to the right until you feel the muscles on one side of the neck stretching.
- Hold for five seconds; then slowly turn head toward the left side and repeat the process. Face front again.

Figure 11–3   Shoulder Stretch

- Next, bring your head up and back so you are looking up to the ceiling. Feel this stretch in the muscles under the chin and in the front part of the neck. Hold for five seconds.
- Now lower chin toward your chest. This stretches the muscles in the back part of the neck. After five seconds, bring head up straight once again and relax.

Next come the *grimace stretch* and *jaw stretch*.

- Squint eyes and tighten as many facial muscles as you can into "a wrinkled face." Hold for five seconds, relax and repeat for five more seconds.
- Clench teeth together as if biting down on something. Hold for five seconds. Now relax and let jaws hang open. Repeat two more times.

We'll finish off the stamina stretches with the *forehead stretch.*

- Raise eyebrows as if surprised. Tighten forehead mus-

cles as much as possible. Hold for five seconds and
then relax.

- Lower eyebrows and tighten forehead into a frown.
  Hold this expression for five seconds and then relax.

After the stamina stretches are finished, take two slow,
deep breaths as described earlier. Keep your arms down by
your sides and take in as much air as you can. Slowly
exhale and relax. Notice the life returning to your muscles
from the stretching.

Review:

1. Rope climb—40 seconds
2. Reach for the stars—15 seconds (repeat 3 times)
3. Shoulder stretch—10 seconds (repeat 3 times)
4. Neck stretch—20 seconds (repeat 4 times)
5. Grimace stretch—5 seconds (repeat 2 times)
6. Forehead stretch—5 seconds (repeat 2 times)

PHASE 3: ENERGY-IN-MOTION

Time to complete: Five minutes

Purpose: To reoxygenate the blood; relax and strengthen
your muscles; and restore cardiopulmonary vitality.

Description:

Now your body is starting to get revitalized. The energy-
in-motion routine is designed to take you to your energy
peak. The total routine takes only five minutes to complete.
All exercises are done standing up and are moderate in
intensity so they won't overheat you when you do them in
your business clothes.

Remember, the goal is energy. *This is not a physical fitness routine:* You don't want to strain muscles. if you exercise a lot, you may have a tendency to want to increase the intensity or repetitions of these energy-in-motion exercises. You must remember that the goal is primarily *revitalization*, *not* strength and fitness. Keep the pace smooth and gentle.

Begin with the *arm circles* exercise.

- Stand straight with arms extended out to the sides. Keeping elbows straight, rotate both arms in small clockwise circles. With each movement make circles bigger and bigger. Continue for 10 repetitions.

- Pause, reverse directions and do 10 clockwise expanding circles. Keep a moderate to brisk pace. As you proceed, imagine energy flowing into every part of body.

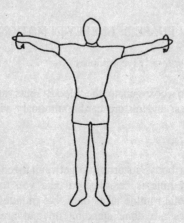

Figure 11-4   Arm Circles

Now you are ready for the *arm bend-and-extend* exercise.

- Extend arms straight out to each side, palms facing upward. Bend arms at the elbow, bringing hands down onto shoulders. Then extend arms straight out once again.
- Do one full "bend and extend" each second, repeating for 30 seconds. *Breathe freely as you complete this exercise*, taking in as much air as possible.

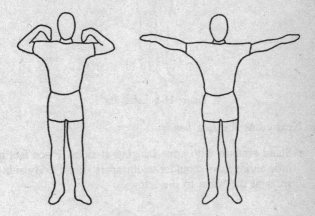

Figure 11–5   Arm Bend-and-Extend

Next let your arms hang down by your sides to prepare for the *arms up* exercise. This exercise is similar to a jumping jack except you do not use your legs.

- Keeping arms straight, swing them upward until hands come together over your head.
- Now quickly bring arms down to sides. Continue for 30 seconds. Each up-and-down movement should take about 2 seconds. Breathe normally.

Figure 11-6   Arms Up

Next come the *side bends*.

• Stand straight with arms hanging at sides. Place feet a little more than shoulder-width apart. Bend body sideways at the waist to the left.

Figure 11-7   Side bends

- Stop when you feel the muscles in your sides stretching out. Keep both feet flat on the floor. Straighten and bend sideways to the right.
- Keep alternating in a smooth, fluid motion. Do not bounce. Keep going until you have completed 10 repetitions on each side.

Now get ready for the *half-squats*. (If you have any problems with your knees, skip this exercise and go on to the next one.) Women wearing high heels should take them off for this and the next exercise.

Figure 11–8   Half-Squats

- Place hands on hips. Bend knees about halfway and sink into a half squat. Do not bend all the way down. Keep your back straight and your heels flat on the floor.
- Now straighten legs and stand erect with slow and smooth movements. If you feel unsteady, rest hands on the back of a chair as you do your half-squat. Do one squat (down and up) every 2 to 3 seconds until you have completed 10 to 15 squats.

We will finish with the *mini-walk*.

- Walk in place or around a small area in your office at a moderate pace. Raise knees and bring arms up slightly as you walk, as if marching in a parade.
- Breathe smoothly, taking in as much air as you need. Continue nonstop for 2½ minutes.

Review:

1. Arm circles—10 repetitions clockwise and counter-clockwise
2. Arm bend and extend—30 repetitions in 30 seconds
3. Arms up—up and down motions for 30 seconds
4. Side bends—10 repetitions on each side
5. Half squats—10 to 15 repetitions
6. Miniwalk—continue for 2½ minutes

Note: remember, all exercises should be moderate in intensity. The goal is energy, not aerobic fitness. You should not be working up a sweat. If you are out of physical condition, try the first three exercises and gradually work your way up to all six.

PHASE 4: BRAIN BOOSTER

Time to complete: Four minutes

Purpose: To refresh and reprogram your tired mind and restimulate your brain.

Description:

Imagery and visualization can help refocus the mind and rekindle powers of concentration. The brain booster routine is designed to reprogram your tired mind so you feel refreshed and ready for more action.

Imagery can have great influence on the unconscious part of the mind. The unconscious can respond to imagined experiences as if they actually happened. So if you vividly imagine yourself full of energy and stamina, your mind starts to believe that you really *are* full of energy and stamina. If you mentally program images of yourself going through the rest of your business day feeling refreshed and revitalized, your mind will believe it and act on those images.

The brain booster routine is relatively simple.

- Sit down. Make yourself comfortable without slouching or lying down. Clear everything from your mind. Concentrate only on the present.
- Say the following words to yourself either out loud or in your mind: "I am feeling strong, alert and refreshed."
- Repeat this slowly, in a *strong, convincing tone*. Do not allow any counterproductive ideas or thoughts to come into your mind. Repeat sentence at least 10 to 15 times.
- Now say "My mind and body are getting stronger and stronger." Repeat 10 to 15 times, *using more force and enthusiasm than before*. As you speak, imagine an inner strength building inside you, causing a tingling in your arms, legs, shoulders and chest.
- Avoid intruding thoughts such as "This is ridiculous, I'm wasting time," or negative thoughts such as "I'm not sure I can close the deal this afternoon." *Feel* the vitality building inside you. Feel it physically, emotionally, and spiritually.
- Finally, say, "*Every part of me is full of positive energy.*" Repeat with force and confidence at least 10 times. Continue to focus on feelings of physical and mental stamina and energy.
- Now take a moment to enjoy the alertness you feel.

Your next task is to energize yourself for the rest of the day by mentally rehearsing every business activity that may come up during the next several hours.

- Check your schedule to see exactly what you will be doing.
- Close your eyes and visualize yourself in each activity. You might be reading a report, reprimanding or encouraging a subordinate, discussing an important issue at a meeting, taking a flight to Chicago, talking on the telephone or dining with clients.
- In each scene, envision yourself at peak efficiency. See yourself going through each task, full of vigor and vitality, at a super level of concentration and energy. You are on top of every issue and decision, you are handling difficult situations with relative ease and your mental and physical resources are boundless.
- Rehearse each activity in your business day.

As you might expect, *concentration* is the key to this routine—you must really put yourself into it. Use all of your powers of imagination and creativity.

You will be amazed at how well this procedure works. In fact, sports psychologists have been teaching world class athletes this type of imagery for years with excellent results.

Review:

1. Close your eyes and concentrate.
2. Repeat "I am feeling strong, alert and refreshed" 10 to 15 times in a strong, convincing tone.
3. Repeat "My mind and body are getting stronger and stronger" 10 to 15 times, using more enthusiasm than before.
4. Conjure up images of strength and power.

5. Repeat "Every part of me is full of positive energy" at least 10 times.

6. Mentally rehearse the remainder of your day's schedule, using images of strength, vigor and stamina.

PHASE 5: POWER SNACK

Time to complete: Four minutes

Purpose: To replenish fluids and supply glucose to your brain and muscles

Description

Now that your muscles and brain are revitalized, supercharge your body's engine with glucose and fluids. *The Hilton Head executive stamina power snack* consists of the following:

- Carbonated water—2 cups (Seltzer, club soda or one of the popular brands of "naturally" carbonated water)
- High energy/high potassium fruit—one portion of any one of the following fruits:

  1 whole medium banana (80 calories)
  1 whole medium orange (80 calories)
  ¼ cup of raisins (115 calories)
  5 dates (100 calories)
  5 dried prunes (100 calories)
  2 cups strawberries (100 calories)
  ½ medium cantaloupe (80 calories)
  ¼ honeydew (80 calories)

The water will help replenish some of the fluids you've lost during the business day. Carbonation speeds the absorption of liquid into your bloodstream and gives you a faster boost than noncarbonated water. *Always include a cold, carbonated beverage in your power snack*. In fact, if the fruit is not available on a particular occasion, drink the carbonated beverage anyway. It will help perk you up even without the fruit. Bottled carbonated drinks flavored naturally with fruit juice and noncaffeinated, low-calorie soft drinks will do if nothing else is available, but the fruit or fruit juice will give you much more of a boost.

Eating the high energy/high potassium fruit provides complex carbohydrates that are absorbed quickly into your system and which will be readily converted into the glucose needed by your body for energy. The potassium in the fruit will help your body conserve fluid over the next several hours.

All of the fruits I have listed contain between 300 mg and 500 mg of potassium per serving. I have equated the fruit portions more in relation to potassium content than calorie level. Even so, as you can see from my list, calories range from 80 to 115. This is a low enough number of calories so that even if you are trying to lose weight, you wouldn't have to worry about weight gain from this power snack.

For many business people, the most practical high-energy fruits to have on hand at the office are bananas, packaged raisins or oranges. These can be easily tucked away into your briefcase on your way out of the house in the morning. If you have access to a refrigerator at work, so much the better; you'll be able to stock it with a variety of the recommended fruits. Or when you go out for lunch, pick up some fruit and bring it back with you for later in the afternoon.

In my experience, most business people want to keep things simple, so they just have a banana or raisins every day. If you don't mind repetition, this might be the best approach for you to take.

Avoid foods containing refined sugar. They merely give you a quick but short-lived lift. You'll crash between one and three hours later when your blood sugar level drops; then you'll feel even more fatigued and lethargic than you've felt all day.

If you want a change of pace and have a little more time, try one of the following drink mixtures that contain both carbonated water and high energy fruit. These drinks can also be substituted for alcoholic beverages when going out for "cocktails."

Super Energy Drink Suggestions

• Add ice and keep these drinks cold.

• Power Plus

Mix in blender:
> 1 banana
> ½ cup fresh strawberries
> 1 cup sparkling water
> Chopped ice

• Bloody Energizer

Mix in glass with ice:
> 8 oz tomato juice or V-8
> 4 oz sparkling water

Note: If you need to restrict your salt intake, avoid drinks with tomato juice bases.

• Stamina Screwdriver

Mix in glass with ice:
>   8 oz orange juice
>   4 oz sparkling water

• Strawberry Surprise

Mix in blender:
>   ½ cup fresh strawberries
>   1 oz papaya juice
>   2 oz apple juice
>   4 oz sparkling water

• Grapefruit Spritzer

Mix in glass with ice:
>   8 oz grapefruit juice
>   4 oz sparkling water

More Hilton Head Power-Snack Ideas

Here are some additional power-snack suggestions that require more preparation time. All of these should be accompanied by seltzer or other sparkling water.

• Executive Gorp

Hikers and mountain climbers often eat something called *gorp* for energy on the trail. Gorp consists of a mixture of seeds, nuts and dried fruit. Here's a simple version for the person in business.

Mix in a bowl, cup or plastic bag:
>¼ cup raisins
>¼ cup sunflower seeds
>¼ cup peanuts, unsalted, dry roasted

• Banana Boost

Mix in cup or bowl:
>1 medium banana, sliced
>½ cup sliced strawberries
>Top with 1 tablespoon plain yogurt

• Fruit Mix

Mix in cup or bowl:
>3 medium apricots
>½ medium apple, cored and sliced
>¼ cantaloupe, cubed
>2 figs

• Breakfast in the p.m.

Mix in bowl:
>¾ oz raisin bran
>½ cup low-fat (2%) milk

Eat cereal along with a mixture of 4-oz orange juice and 4-oz sparkling water.

• Orange Blossom

Mix and sprinkle with coconut and artificial sweetener, if desired:

> 1 medium orange, sectioned
> 1 medium grapefruit, sectioned

Overview

Remember, your *resting-in-motion* routine must be practiced regularly to be effective. You'll be amazed at how much of a boost it will give you for the rest of the day. It may be the most important 20 minutes you spend at work!

12

▼

The Three-Minute Mini-Refresher

If you structure your time well, on most days you should have no problem in scheduling the resting-in-motion routine. On some days, however, travel and/or meetings may put you on an extremely tight schedule. I'm sure you have had days when you can't spare even 15 to 20 minutes.

On busy days you can use the *three-minute mini-refresher* routine. Unlike the full resting-in-motion sequence, the mini-routine consists of three short phases:

1. The breath of life
2. Quick body/mind refresher
3. The stamina drink

To concentrate on the mini-refresher, you must get off by yourself for three minutes. Wait for an appropriate break in the proceedings. If you are in charge of a meeting, suggest a five-minute break. During breaks, executives have a tendency to continue to discuss business. You must avoid such conversations and find a private space quickly. If you are with an important client, excuse yourself to sign critical paperwork or make an essential phone call. If you are away from your workplace and meeting in a hotel, mention that you need to place a call or to pick up something from your room and then go up to your room for your refresher.

The Breath of Life

The goal of this phase of the routine is to force a steady supply of fresh air into your lungs. The ultimate objective is to reduce fatigue by infusing a new supply of oxygen-rich blood. Did you ever see a professional football player breathing deeply into an oxygen mask on the sidelines? He's doing exactly what you are trying to do—regaining stamina for another surge at the competition.

Unlike the full resting-in-motion routine, the mini-routine requires only 60 seconds of deep breathing.

- Stand straight with arms hanging loosely at sides. Breathe slowly and evenly.
- After a few normal breaths, raise both arms up from sides, straight overhead, when you inhale. At the very top of your breath, arms should be stretched overhead with hands touching one another. Hold the breath for two to three seconds, then slowly bring arms back down to sides while exhaling.
- Breathe slowly and easily for 20 seconds, inhaling through nose and exhaling through mouth. Arms should go up and down in a smooth, fluid motion. Don't rush through this routine.
- Rest for 10 seconds with arms at sides. Shake arms loosely to stimulate the muscles.
- Now begin breathing again, raising and lowering your

arms for 30 seconds. Remember, you want *slow, deep, steady* breathing.

The Quick Body/Mind Refresher

This phase of the routine can be completed in about 1/½ minutes once you get the hang of it. It combines simple body movements with a "power of the mind" visualization routine for maximum rejuvenation. By doing the mental and physical elements of this phase *simultaneously*, you can complete the entire sequence in short order. First I'll explain the body movements; then the mental exercises. Just remember to do them both at the same time in actual practice.

Seat yourself comfortably in a chair. Try to use one without rollers since it may move during these exercises. The three mini-routine refresher exercises are body twister, sit-and-walk and rowing in place.

BODY TWISTER

If you have had disk or back problems or if you experience pain in your back, consult your physician before doing any of these exercises.

- Sit straight in the chair with back arched slightly inward. Sit forward enough so body is not resting on the back of the chair. Now bend arms at the elbows and lift them up, clasping hands together on top of head.
- Slowly twist back and forth from side to side, breathing freely and easily as you do so. Go a little faster as you proceed but keep a smooth motion. Stop after 20 seconds and go on to the next body movement.

SIT-AND-WALK

- Sit comfortably in chair. Lift one leg up, bringing thigh up toward body. Put that leg down and bring the other leg up.
- Bring one leg up after the other, doing a sitting-walk with high, exaggerated steps. Start out slowly and then gradually increase pace as you continue. Continue a steady pace for 20 seconds.

ROWING IN PLACE

If you've ever rowed a boat or worked out on a rowing machine, this next movement will be easy.

- While seated, bend arms out to sides as if rowing a boat. Now reach forward as though taking a stroke and then pull back as though pulling the oars through the water.
- Push arms forward once again and repeat the same motion. Your movements should be slow and steady at first. You can pick up a little speed as you continue but keep a rhythm to your stroke. Continue rowing for 20 seconds.

A Quick Mental Vacation

It is extremely important to free your mind of business thoughts during these body movements in order to gain maximum benefit from this mini refresher. Wait until you are finished with the refresher to mull over business matters.

While you begin the body twister, imagine a large metal safe. Now visualize putting all of your business and personal worries, thoughts and concerns in the safe. Don't leave anything out. Remind yourself that no harm will be done by simply not thinking about business for the next minute. In fact, if you're starting to feel fatigue, it's unlikely that you'll come up with any earth-shattering solution to your problems in the next 60 seconds.

Once all these thoughts and concerns are in the safe, "lock" them up securely. Imagine yourself locking several padlocks and wrapping large, heavy chains around the safe. Once you are convinced the safe is locked up tight, put the keys away. You are not avoiding your concerns; you are merely putting them aside temporarily so they won't get in your way.

As you do the sit-and-walk movement, imagine that you actually are walking through a grassy field. Use all of your powers of fantasy so that you really feel as though you are walking through hilly, grassy fields on a sunny day. You are all alone, feeling more energy and stamina with each step you take. Don't allow any other thoughts to get in the way. Lose yourself in the image.

While rowing in place, imagine that you are actually on a quiet lake, lagoon, pond or river. You are all alone, feeling peaceful. With each stroke, you glide through the water. With each stroke, your body and mind feel stronger and more alert. Let your imagination go. Concentrate on images of energy, confidence and stamina. Don't let your mind wander.

When you finish the body movements, imagine the safe once again. See yourself unlocking the chains and opening up the safe. Remove all of your thoughts and concerns, but this time imagine that you are a lot stronger than before. View these concerns not as problems, but as challenges that you can't wait to take on.

The Stamina Drink

Since you have only one minute left, you probably won't have time to eat the power snack described in the full resting-in-motion routine. A stamina drink will serve the same purpose when you are pinched for time. You may have to arrange ahead of time for this to be ready at your break, otherwise, you can easily get it at a snack bar, restaurant or cocktail lounge. Cold drinks may be served at your meeting during the break. In that case, so much the better.

Your stamina drink should consist of:

- Carbonated water—4 oz
- Orange juice—8 oz

Mix these two together and drink cold, with a lot of ice. In a pinch, either one alone will do. This won't be quite as good as the combination, but it will help a great deal.

Resting-in-Motion Versus the Mini-Refresher

Use the mini-refresher only when you simply cannot find time for the full resting-in-motion routine. The full routine will revive you more completely. The more shortcuts you take, the less my total system will help you. I want you to have *maximum* stamina. Many of the managers I deal with have to experience the results of the Hilton Head executive stamina program before they believe it. This is why you must be consistent, especially in the beginning of the program. I guarantee you'll be delighted with your new-found stamina!

13

▼

Taking
Business Trips
in Stride

One of the most grueling and energy-draining features of the corporate world is the business trip. Since I am consulted by many international business people, I am acutely aware of how long-distance travel robs your body of stamina. Yet, with some executives travel is a way of life.

One of my clients, the general manager of international operations for a large electronics firm, logs over 100,000 miles every year and travels to such places as Saudi Arabia, New Zealand and China. Before he put my program into practice, his travel schedule was taking a heavy toll on his life. Once at his destination he usually felt completely fatigued and even disoriented by jet lag. Of course, this affected his business dealings. In the past, when he was traveling less, he had been able to handle it better and tough it out. Traveling 100,000 miles a year, however, is a much more formidable task than the 15,000 miles he had been logging before.

Finally, the president of the company realized that his general manager's work efficiency was failing, and sent him to me. The president was genuinely worried. He was watching a valuable employee waste away before his eyes and felt that the company was to blame. (Many companies are taking a much more active interest in their employees' health and stamina.)

Within a few short weeks, his general manager was putting my stamina travel plan into operation with great success. Better planning of his time and delegating authority to others enabled him to reduce travel by about 25%. This still meant a lot of miles in the air; with the aid of the program, however, those miles were spent in self-rejuvenation. He now arrives at his destinations refreshed and ready for action.

You, too, can discover the same results. In this chapter, you will learn how you can actually use business travel to your advantage, so that it becomes a positive challenge rather than an exhausting drudgery.

What Causes Travel Fatigue?

Travel fatigue is due, in part, to the same six executive fatigue factors described in Chapter 3. One of the most obvious contributors is muscle cramping from sitting a long time in a confined seat. Although first class and business class seats are roomier, a few hours spent sitting in any of them may convince you that airplane seats were not designed with regular-size human beings in mind.

Fluid loss is another major culprit in sapping your stamina on business flights. The dry air-conditioning on airplanes dramatically speeds the loss of moisture from your skin. Because they act as diuretics, the coffee, tea, colas and alcohol served in flight further dehydrate you. You can lose up to *three pounds* of water from your body during a long flight. Loss of that much water in such a short time is fatiguing because your body cells require water for the proper metabolism and transport of nutrients that provide energy.

On cross-country or international flights, jet lag is a third influence on your energy level. Changing time zones rapidly can disrupt sleeping and eating patterns, disorganize thinking patterns and give you an overall groggy, listless feeling. Your body's releases of hormones (thyroid-stimulating hormone and adrenocorticotrophic hormone) and brain neurotransmitters (norepinephrine and serotonin) do not parallel the time of day and night outside. These substances, which affect your wake/sleep cycle, drowsiness and emotional ups-and-downs, normally follow a clear-cut circadian rhythm (daily body cycle). Such cycles do not change rapidly, so a five-hour time zone change requires at least three days for your "body clock" to reset itself.

There are ways, however, to adjust more rapidly or even to fool your body into thinking you haven't changed time zones at all! My travel secrets are being used daily by executives who have graduated from the Hilton Head program. These very same executives once thought, as perhaps you do, that fatigue during business trips is inevitable. Well, you can win the battle over jet lag and I'm going to show you how.

What to Do Before You Leave

Having a plan of action for your business trip is a key to keeping your stamina level high. We use an adage at the Institute that applies to travel as well as to any area of business life: IF YOU FAIL TO PLAN, YOU ARE PLANNING TO FAIL!

My pre-trip planning guide requires you to consider the following:

1. Schedule your time before you leave.

Before you leave, give serious thought to your schedule at your destination. Depending on your position in the company and the nature of your business, you may or may not have very much control of this schedule. Try to arrange for 30-60 minutes either early or late in the day for your exercise time.

In addition, you will need 20 minutes in the late afternoon or early evening for my resting-in-motion routine. If you have a very busy schedule with one meeting after another, insist on a 30-minute break to refresh yourself. If need be, say that you must use this time to brief your staff at home or to follow up on other business. If at all possible, try not to schedule business discussions at all of your meals. Arrange to have one or two meals per day by yourself or, at least, engaged in conversations that are not related to the business at hand. I know you want to get as much business in as possible, but you must pace yourself. By giving your mind periodic breaks, you'll be improving your concentration and mental acuity.

2. Leave town early.

I realize that you must fit business travel into an already busy schedule but, if possible, try to leave town a day earlier than usual. This is especially true if you are traveling through time zones and you will be gone for three or more days. If you'll be gone only a day or two, it doesn't matter if you leave early or not, but do so if you can. Your body will thank you for it.

By arriving a day before your business begins, you have a longer time to adjust to the new time zone and to recover from the flight. Take work with you if you like. You don't have to spend this extra day relaxing, I just want your body there a little early so you'll have time to get on a schedule, exercise and become used to your surroundings.

Don't tell anyone at your destination that you'll be arriving early—they'll push up all of your meetings and start business early. Tell them you'll make your own arrangements to get to the hotel and meetings since you are not sure exactly when you'll be arriving. You don't need to offer lengthy explanations.

There are occasions, however, when this strategy may be difficult or even inappropriate. You may be making an extremely important trip and the VIPs at the other end may insist on meeting you upon your arrival. Or, if your business is in the Orient where courtesy is vital, your arriving a day early without telling anyone might be considered rude. Under these circumstances, say that you have had a hectic schedule over the past few days, weren't able to sleep well and desperately need rest before any social or business get-togethers. Conveying this message prior to your arrival will keep you schedule clear for the first few hours or perhaps even the first day.

3. Pack appropriately for your stamina routines.

Be sure to pack a few casual clothes and shoes appropriate for walking. A former client, who was in the diplomatic service, once sheepishly offered this explanation of why she had failed to exercise on a business trip: "I opened my suitcase on the first night in Madrid and realized I had not packed my jogging shoes. I gave up my exercise plan then and there and decided I would have to wait until I returned home to do the stamina stride. I know that sounds like a dumb excuse but I felt, at the time, that if I couldn't do it right, as I had planned it, I couldn't do it at all. I realize now how illogical that was."

When you are rushed and under the stress of a business

trip it is very easy to fall into this all-or-nothing thinking. This is why it's important to pack the right clothes and shoes—just looking at those shoes will remind you of exercise. Take your walking or running shoes even if you are only going away overnight. You never know when you might find some spare time.

Also remember that you don't need the "right" shoes or clothes for exercise. You can walk in any clothes, and the resting-in-motion routine is designed for people wearing business clothes.

4. Eat less and exercise more before you leave.

For a full 24 hours before you leave, eat more lightly than normal. If your trip will be a transcontinental one, start eating lighter meals 48 hours in advance. Your body can adjust faster to travel if you have cleansed your engine of excess fuel.

To ensure maximum travel-readiness, I suggest you follow Food plan 3—Weight loss plan (refer to Chapter 5) for the 24 to 48 hours before a business trip, whether or not you are trying to lose weight. On the day of the trip and the day of arrival, you can follow whichever of my nutritional plans you have been on. Try to eat a little lighter than normal, however. I would rather you ate five or six light meals than one or two heavy ones during travel.

There is a nutritional program that is touted as a jet-lag diet, in which you drastically vary your carbohydrate and protein consumption before and during travel. Changing the nutritional composition of your diet can upset your system and may actually be counterproductive. In my experience, your stamina will be maintained and improved by following the Hilton Head nutritional plans that I have outlined for you and by remembering to eat more moderately than usual.

Since you will be sitting in a small seat during your trip and your muscles will be cramped, it is wise to get in as much walking and stretching as possible in the 24 to 48 hours *before* you board the plane. Try to double the amount of exercise for the two days prior to your flight. On the day of the flight, get up earlier than usual and go off for a 30- to 45-minute stamina stride. I'll give you a more detailed, step-by-step method of avoiding jet lag later in this chapter.

5. Stay in a "stamina hotel."

No, I'm not starting a new hotel chain patterned after my Hilton Head Health Institute (although, come to think of it, that may be a great solution to the stamina problems of business travelers)! By "stamina hotel," I mean a hotel that will make it easier for you to stick to my program. When you, your assistant or travel agent makes your reservations, choose a hotel that:

- Is situated in an area that is conducive to walking, such as one that is near a park or in a low-crime neighborhood.
- Has in-house exercise facilities and equipment such as a swimming pool, exercycles or treadmills.
- Serves a varied menu with special, healthy meals that are low in salt, cholesterol and sugar.
- Has 24-hour room service or an in-room mini-refrigerator for your stamina snack.

If you are traveling abroad, it may be a little more difficult to obtain information on these matters. Try to get as much input as possible from the company or executives you will be doing business with as to which hotels in the area might qualify as "stamina hotels."

These criteria are getting easier to meet as hotels around

the world are changing their facilities in response to health-minded business travelers. A major new hotel complex is seldom built now without exercise facilities.

Hyatt and Marriott hotels are in the forefront of this change and would receive a four-star rating in my list of "stamina hotels." Hyatt is rapidly expanding fitness facilities in all of their hotels and even publishes a directory listing which of their hotels have exercise amenities. Marriott hotels offer a "Good for You" menu, which consists of meals that are low in fat, salt and cholesterol.

How to Boost Stamina During Your Flight

There are certain secrets to increasing stamina during your flight that are essential for your success with this program. You must be alert to the following in-flight factors.

1. Seating

In order to have as much access to movement as possible during your flight, choose an aisle seat. Aisle seating enables you to get in and out easily, allowing you to move around the plane and do the exercises that are part of my resting-in-motion routine.

Make sure you sit in the nonsmoking section even if you are a smoker. You'll breathe easier and take in a better supply of oxygen. If you smoke, you can make occasional visits to the back of the plane to light up.

If at all possible, travel first- or business-class. This is probably not possible unless you are at a certain level in the company; however, on very crucial trips you should insist on it, using the argument that you are an important company asset and your state of mind and body when you arrive are essential to the successful completion of the deal. Have confidence in yourself!

About an hour into the flight take a tour of the plane, looking for two or three unoccupied seats in a row. Then move there so you can stretch out across the seats to avoid muscle cramping. This strategy also helps to give you more foot room because you can move any under-seat baggage next to you.

If your company sends you on their own private plane, so much the better. Many of the executives with whom I deal fly privately, so they can walk around, stretch out or do what they please during the flight. Even if you are flying coach, there are things you can do to ensure a high level of stamina. Make the best of your situation and realize that you will soon be moving up the corporate ladder to more and more travel options.

2. Special meals

Here is one of the cardinal rules of my program that you must never forget: *Never, ever eat the standard meals served by the airlines*. You must *always* order a special meal every time you take a business flight. As long as you order a special meal 24 hours in advance, you will have no trouble getting what you want. Most major airlines offer several special meals including low fat, low calorie, low salt, diabetic, vegetarian and many others. Because fewer of these meals are prepared, they are always tastier than the standard fare. In addition, they usually are healthier and more in line with the nutritional guidelines for stamina that I have set down for you.

I suggest you order the vegetarian meals when you fly. In doing so you will be getting a low-fat, high-carbohydrate meal that will help to maintain your stamina level.

Order every meal this way. If the flight is short and only a snack is served, you won't be able to order a special selection. In that case, have an apple or banana in your briefcase and order orange juice and carbonated water.

Remember too that you don't have to eat a meal just because it's served to you. I'm always amazed at how people on planes eat, not because they are hungry, but simply because it's being served. *Do not* eat an airline meal just because you are bored or because you're trying to get your money's worth.

3. Fluids

Throughout the flight, make sure you are drinking enough fluids. *Decline all caffeinated and alcoholic beverages.* There should be no exceptions to this rule. If you are flying first class, refuse the complimentary cocktails and wine. If your flight is delayed on the runway and the airlines offers you a free drink to compensate, refuse it. If you are under a lot of tension and feel you need a drink to relax, don't order one. This kind of relaxation will not help you.

Instead, keep a steady supply of power drinks coming. Drink lots of carbonated water either alone or with orange juice. When the attendant first comes around, order two carbonated drinks and an orange juice. Then try to get more about every hour. I am serious about this: Fluid replacement is crucial to your maintaining a high stamina level and arriving fresh.

4. In-flight resting-in-motion

During long flights your muscles will tire from sheer inactivity. About once every hour and a half, you'll need to stretch them out.

The best way to rejuvenate your whole body during the flight is to do a slightly modified version of the resting-in-motion routines outlined in Chapters 11 and 12. The only modification needed with my 20-minute routine would be the elimination of the energy-in-motion phase. These exercises would be difficult for you to do in the cramped quarters of an airplane. Instead, substitute a five-minute walk around the cabin or try the sit-and-walk routine that's part of my shorter three minute resting-in-motion sequence.

Because of cramped quarters and passenger traffic in the aisles, your walk around the cabin will be slow. You can still give your muscles a workout by exaggerating the muscle tightness in your legs with every stride. Concentrate on tensing all of the leg muscles from buttocks to toes as you take each step.

On a cross-country flight, you should rest-in-motion at least twice; on a transcontinental flight, you should go through this routine at least three or four times, spaced over the length of the flight. Sometimes it takes a bit of planning to avoid the food and drink carts that take up the width of the aisle. Most cabin attendants prefer that you remain in your seat; with proper timing, however, you can complete your resting-in-motion routine with little bother to anyone. If you are self-conscious, go into the restroom and do the reach-for-the-stars, rope climb and half-squats described in Chapters 10 and 11.

I have found in-flight resting-in-motion to be contagious. I'll never forget the time I was flying to England for a book publicity tour and I found myself leading a group of about eight people in my stamina exercises. While seated, I began the breath-of-life phase of my routine. The fellow across the aisle from me asked me what I was doing and as I explained resting-in-motion to him, several of the passengers around us became intrigued with the conversation.

"That's exactly what I need," one woman exclaimed. "I'm always so tired from traveling," she continued.

Not only did several of us go through the routine together, but on the next go-around for beverages the stewardess was faced with eight orders for orange juice and carbonated water! Believe me, I don't usually lead in-flight exercise classes. I just find business travelers so eager to learn the secrets of stamina that it doesn't take much explanation to turn them into disciples of the Hilton Head Executive Stamina Program.

Delays

Use any delay time in airports to your advantage. As soon as you are informed of the status of your plane, take the following steps:

- Lock your hand luggage in a locker to make walking easier.
- Take a 30- to 60-minute moderately paced walk through the airport, or, better yet, go outside and walk around the area (at some airports this may not be possible due to traffic congestion).
- Go to the airport restaurant or bar and order the power snack described in Chapter 11.
- If you are a member of one of the airline special executive waiting rooms, find a quiet corner or one of the small workrooms that some of them have, and take 20 minutes to do the resting-in-motion routine.

What to Do When You Arrive

Unless you have a meeting immediately upon arrival, go straight to your hotel. In your room, change into loose, comfortable clothes and go through my resting-in-motion routine once again. Then take a bath or shower and put on fresh clothing. I would also advise that you spend 30–60 minutes out in the daylight, especially after a very long flight. Although the exact reasons remain unclear, exposure to daylight may help your biological clock readjust faster to a new time zone.

Do not try to sleep until you have completed this routine. If you arrive late at night, do the resting-in-motion routine; then bathe or shower and go to bed. Get up early and get out for a 30- to 60-minute stamina stride the next morning.

If you're arriving in another country early in the morning and your biological clock tells you it is the middle of the night, follow the sequence of events I have just described, and then sleep for two hours. If you cannot sleep, at least lie down and relax for two hours. Then go to sleep again at your usual time of night (appropriate to your new time zone).

Soon after your arrival, check with the hotel to make sure you will be able to have a steady supply of carbonated water and orange juice. Also order a basket of fresh fruit for your room.

Check the hotel menu for items compatible with the Hilton Head executive nutrition plan. Special items are not usually needed, since most of the foods on my nutrition plan are quite easy to obtain just about anywhere. That's what makes this system so easy to follow.

If you are in a city in the United States, call the local chapter of the American Heart Association. Many restaurants throughout the country are cooperating with a new nation-wide health program by serving one or two low-fat, low-cholesterol, low-sodium meals recommended by the Heart Association. Most local chapters can provide you with a list of restaurants involved in this program. These special menu items will make it easier for you to choose healthier, "stamina" foods.

During your stay, make certain you follow my nutrition, exercise and resting-in-motion plan to the letter. Do not use a busy schedule or your out-of-town status as an excuse to stop your energy routine. My program will give you the stamina that is absolutely necessary to keep you at your peak, especially when away from home. Once you use it a few times on business trips, you'll be living the stamina lifestyle without even thinking about it. The rewards will be so great you'll never want to give it up.

Taking the Lag Out of Jet Lag

In addition to the plan of attack I have outlined so far, you may want to use these special strategies to prevent or reduce jet lag when your trip takes you through several time zones. Here are my secrets for overcoming jet lag:

1. Reset your biological clock before you leave.

You can begin the process of adjustment to your new time zone even before you leave on your trip. It will take about three days to accomplish this change. You probably won't be able to totally reset your clock in three days, but it will give you a terrific head start.

If you are flying *west*, follow this schedule for three days prior to your trip:

- On the first night go to bed 30 minutes later than your usual bedtime. Then move your bedtime back 30 minutes more on the second night. Repeat this procedure on the third night so that after three days you are retiring 1½ hours later than normal.
- On the first morning get up 30 minutes later than usual. Extend your wake up time by 30 minutes more each morning for the next two days. (This is, of course, much easier to do on a week-end rather than workdays.)
- Eat each of your regular meals 30 minutes later than

normal on the first day, moving them back by 30 minutes each day. (If this strategy is too difficult to follow, eat four or five small meals at regular intervals and avoid alcoholic beverages.)

If you are flying east, simply reverse the process.

- Beginning on the first day go to bed 30 minutes earlier than usual. Then move your bedtime 30 minutes earlier on the second night. Repeat this procedure on the third night so that after three days you are retiring 1½ hours earlier than normal.
- If your work schedule permits, get up 30 minutes earlier than usual on the first morning. Wake up earlier by 30 minutes more each morning for the next two days. If this is not possible because of your work hours, try to make your wake-up time at least 15 minutes earlier each morning.
- Eat each of your regular meals 30 minutes earlier than normal on the first day, moving them back by 30 minutes each day.

2. Consider staying on your own time.

If you are going to be gone for only a day or two, you might consider staying on your own time no matter what time it is where you are. A real estate mogul who attended my Hilton Head Health Institute stays on his own time no matter where he does business. Because of his power and influence, he can schedule business appointments at 4:00 a.m. with no objections from anyone.

I'm not suggesting you would be able to do the same thing, but you might if there were less discrepancy between your home time and the time in the city in which you were doing business. For example, if you had a flight from Los

Angeles to New York scheduled to arrive at 7:00 o'clock in the evening Los Angeles time (your body's time), you could feasibly schedule an 11:00 p.m. meeting New York time leaving yourself enough local transit time.

If you decide to stay on your own biological clock's time, it is important to stick to your home-time sleeping and eating schedule as much as possible. On your New York trip, this might mean eating breakfast at 10:00 a.m., lunch at 3:00 p.m., your stamina snack at 6:00 p.m. and dinner at 10:00 p.m.

3. Use your imagination to help you adjust.

Your imagination can be a powerful tool in overcoming jet lag. If your trip is long enough so that you are going to be adjusting to the new time, begin as early as possible to program your mind. As soon as you board the plane set your watch to the new time and begin to think of yourself on that time.

Check the "new" time every 30 minutes; then close your eyes and imagine what you might be doing at that time during a typical day at home. If you would be getting up in the morning and heading to the office, imagine every little detail of your actions. Avoid thoughts of your "old" or biological time. If you are served breakfast on the plane at a time that is near lunchtime according to your watch, imagine you are having lunch. Keep your mind totally on the new time.

If you conjure up these images vividly enough, your body and mind can actually start to believe that the new time *is* your biological time. Remember, the subconscious is easily fooled. It believes anything you tell it as long as you tell it firmly enough and often enough.

Be a Stamina Traveler

Start putting the Hilton Head executive stamina program into action on your very next trip and I guarantee you'll feel like a new person. I've had executives tell me that by using these methods, business trips are now a source of challenge and revitalization for them.

Just keep in mind that my program can be put into practice whether you are at your own office or out on the road. It is practical, because it was developed exclusively for the type of lifestyle you lead.

So be a stamina traveler, and I'll look forward to walking with you up and down the aisles and toasting you with a stamina cocktail on your next flight!

14

▼

The Four Executive Stamina Types

In helping top executives reach their stamina potentials over the years, I have discovered four *executive stamina types* that are most in need of the program. Each differs in his or her approach to business but each shares a common complaint—lack of energy and vitality.

In addition to needing the nutrition and fitness elements of the program, these people also need a change in *attitude*, a change in their basic way of viewing themselves in relation to their business lives. This new way of thinking is what I call the *stamina attitude*. Without it you may read this book, put some of my advice into practice, and within a few short weeks, fall right back into your old habits and become your old listless self again. *I'm not going to let that happen to you.*

Before I tell you about the stamina attitude, see if you recognize yourself in any of these four executive categories:

1. The Sprinter

The sprinter is the all-out executive type: hard-driving, achievement-oriented and competitive. This type is energetic in the short term, but puts so much energy into work that performance tends to be erratic. The sprinter is governed by an all-or-nothing principle: Either give the task at hand 110% or nothing at all.

This dichotomous style shows up in work, family life and health. The sprinter is either giving total effort to a nutrition and exercise regimen or none at all. There is no middle of the road for this executive.

You are a sprinter if you:

- Put off projects longer than you should and then spend three days doing nothing else in order to get the work done.
- Find yourself spending a good amount of time with your spouse and children one week and none the next.
- Get impatient with the lack of drive and initiative in others.
- Want to make it to the top faster than anyone in the history of your company.
- Become anxious when things do not go according to your time schedule.
- Prefer to work and live in the "fast lane."
- Find yourself doing extra work to impress superiors or to set an example for those around you.
- Find yourself racing against the clock to get even the most trivial jobs done.
- Always try to do two things at once, such as eating while working, to get as much accomplished as possible.

The sprinter accomplishes a great deal but is very susceptible to frequent burnouts. He or she actually thrives on stress; however, frequent periods of low energy and stamina result in reduced overall efficiency.

2. The Decathlete

Like the athlete involved in several events, the decathlete executive tries to juggle a lot of different responsibilities. This type is often extremely conscientious and experiences self-doubt and guilt if unable to be everything to everyone.

You are a decathlete if you:

- Try to do all things for all people.
- Set very high goals for yourself and are never satisfied even when you reach them.
- Take on more responsibilities even after promising yourself not to tackle more projects.
- Feel torn, as far as your time is concerned, between work, family, friends, organizations and community activities.
- Feel like you are giving a lot more in life than you are getting.
- Feel that you never have time for yourself.
- Have trouble delegating authority and would rather do the work yourself to make sure it gets done "right."

Decathletes put others' needs first and do more than their share, sometimes to the point of feeling cheated in life.

They rarely have time to take care of themselves. They eat poorly, exercise infrequently and suffer from chronic fatigue. When they do something for themselves to enhance health or stamina, such as exercising, they feel vaguely guilty and wonder whether they could be spending the time more constructively.

3. The Long-Distance Runner

This executive type is a hard worker, but does not keep the frantic, erratic pace of the sprinter. Outwardly he is efficient and in control, but inwardly the days, weeks and years of a fast-paced business life take their toll. Long-distance runners are slowly burning out from years of steady work. Although they do not take on more than they can handle, they fail to take care of their greatest resource—themselves.

You are a long distance runner if you:

• Rarely or never take a vacation.
• Rarely complain about your workload.
• Are even-tempered.
• Tend to internalize stress and suppress your frustrations.
• Are ambitious but have to force yourself to be hard-driving.
• Enjoy challenge, but on a personal rather than a head-to-head competitive level.

Long-distance runners are steady but unrelenting in their careers. In general, they are content with their lives, although over the years their relentless pace takes its toll on their stamina.

These types don't even realize what is happening. Rather, they simply accept falling asleep on the sofa at 9:30 p.m. as a normal part of a manager's life. Long-distance runners do not exercise or pay much attention to nutrition, and rarely admit stress.

These types will go on this way until changes are forced on them by a spouse or an immediate medical concern, such as high blood pressure.

4. The Spectator

Whereas the sprinter and long-distance runner may end up with burnout, the spectator suffers from "rust-out." This person has lost all motivation and joy in work life. Spectators may be stagnating because of a dead-end job, a dissatisfaction with the type of career they are in, or because they have reached a certain level of success and don't know where to go from there.

You are a spectator if you:

- Experience little or no job satisfaction from specific work activities that you once found enjoyable.
- Find that your work life lacks challenge and meaning.
- Feel that you have trouble relating to the concerns and experiences of others at work.
- Feel that you are just living your life from day to day.
- Feel bored and restless with your work and home life.

The spectator is no longer part of the action. Energy and stamina are totally lacking. While spectators may want a more energetic, challenging life, they feel a sense of hopelessness and helplessness. Spectators often want to get back their lost vigor but don't know how to go about it.

The Stamina Attitude

If any of these descriptions comes even close to fitting you, you must learn to develop the *stamina attitude*. It will make your life more fulfilling and vital, and it will help you develop the motivation needed to reap the fullest benefits from the program.

How I Discovered the Stamina Attitude

Several years ago I took a golf lesson from an older, experienced golf pro. I had been badly hooking the ball, spending more of my day in the woods searching for poorly hit shots than on the links.

"Tell me what I am doing wrong so I can correct my mistake," I requested.

Saying nothing, the seasoned veteran instructed me to hit a few balls. The first five were terrible, veering off to the left (as usual). I kept waiting for him to correct my grip, my stance or my swing. Still nothing. On my sixth shot, I hit a tremendous drive, straight and perfect in every respect.

"That's what I've been waiting for!" he shouted excitedly.

I wondered why he was waiting for a good shot when I wanted him to help me with my poor ones.

"Now tell me what you did right. How did you hit such a good shot?" he asked.

"What I did *right*?" I wondered.

I had never really paid much attention to what I did to hit a *good* shot. I was always trying to figure out what I was doing wrong.

After I explained this to him, my golfing guru smiled knowingly and said, "That's why your game is so inconsistent. You don't know enough about what you are doing right when you hit a good shot. You probably attribute straight shots to good luck or chance, thereby concluding that you have little control over making it happen again. On the other hand, you pay a great deal of attention to what is causing your bad shots. And, unlike good shots, you don't attribute hooks and slices to bad luck but to your own incompetence."

Needless to say, he spent the rest of my lesson emphasizing what I was doing correctly. Not once did he mention what I was doing wrong. And, you know, within an hour I was hitting one straight shot after another. To this day I don't know what I was doing wrong. And I don't care to, because I now know what it takes for me to make a good shot.

After reading this book, you certainly know the mechanics of what it takes to put more stamina into your corporate life. You know how and what to eat, how and when to exercise and how to boost your energy level with the exercise routines outlined in previous chapters. You even know why these techniques counteract fatigue and enhance stamina. There's a big difference, however, between knowing what to do and actually doing it each day to ensure maximum stamina and energy.

Haven't you occasionally been in a frame of mind when making healthy life-style choices is easy? When no temptation, no matter how great, seems to faze you? Yet there are other times when eating nutritionally and exercising for more energy seem extremely difficult and agonizing: You may be too busy, or an unexpected crisis may arise.

I want to share with you the attitude that sets the stage for doing everything right. Just as my golf instructor led me down the *positive* path to success, I will do the same for you by sharing the *stamina attitude*.

How to Achieve the Stamina Attitude

The stamina attitude is a way of thinking and perceiving life that gives you strength and power. It is also a way of thinking about yourself and your career that enables you to control and overcome job stress.

To have the stamina attitude you must:

1. Believe that your stamina or lack of it is solely your responsibility.

Let me pose an important question to you: who do you believe is in control of your life?

People tend to be either "external" or "internal" in their response to this question. Executives who are "external" believe that energy and stamina (and many other aspects of their lives, for that matter) exist independently of their own efforts and are, for the most part, beyond their personal control. They feel that the achievement of a healthier, more energetic life is a function of a variety of external factors such as circumstance, emotions, luck, other people, doctors or high-potency vitamin capsules.

If you are an "internal" person, you believe that you and you alone are responsible for your stamina level. Circumstances, schedules, emotions and other people influence your health habits *only if you allow them to affect you*.

To be successful with my system you must become more internal than external. We probably all fall somewhere between these two extremes. You may be internal with some issues in your life but external with others. I'm amazed at how top-level executives can be totally in charge of their business affairs and take full responsibility for their actions but then feel totally out of control when it comes to taking charge of their bodies, their physical health and the health of their personal relationships.

A notable trait of "internal" people is that they strongly believe in the *power of choice*. They believe that it is their choice to stay overtired or to find more energy; it is their choice to eat stamina-draining foods or stamina-enhancing foods; and it is their choice to rest-in-motion or to sit and stew about it. No one is forcing you to do any of these things. When offered a tempting alcoholic drink or pie à la mode (both energy drainers) before an important business conference, *do not* say, "I'd love to have it but the program I'm following won't allow it" or "I'm not supposed to have it." This is "external" thinking. As an internal thinker, you can do whatever you choose to do; so say instead, "No thank you, I've decided not to have any." *You* alone are choosing not to have it. My program is not forcing you to do anything; I have only shown you the way so that you can make your own choices. If you want more stamina, you can have it, but you don't *have* to, if you choose not to.

I want *you* to take full credit for your new, more energetic life. You are the one who will be putting my program to work, so you should be the one to feel good about your efforts.

2. Believe that you have the ability to control your energy and stamina.

Once you take responsibility for determining your stamina level, you must also believe yourself *capable* of accomplishing your stamina goals. Executives who succeed with my program strongly believe that they have the techniques and skills necessary to overcome business fatigue. This expectation of success is known as *self-mastery.*

A fine example of self-mastery is found in the attitude of Eric Heiden, the 21-year-old American speed skater who won 5 gold medals in the 1980 Olympics in Lake Placid, New York. During one of his races Eric actually fell down a few seconds after the start. Not only did he get back up, but he went on to win the race. On a televised interview after his victory, Eric was asked why he got up after falling, why he didn't just give up. His reply was simple and straightforward:

"Because I knew I could still win."

You must gain this much confidence in your abilities to increase your energy and stamina. Otherwise, when you "fall" during the business day because of stress, deadlines or an overly crowded schedule, you won't get back up. You'll drag your fatigued body through the rest of the business day, doing "the best you can" under the circumstances, or you'll go completely off your stamina routine because you think that one slip-up means you've botched the whole day's plan. The Eric Heiden executive would fight back. He would go off by himself, methodically perform the resting-in-motion routine and then plan his stamina strategy for the rest of the day.

This sense of self-mastery grows from "success" experiences. The more you live the program in this book, the more automatic it will become and the more you will believe that you can boost your stamina level. You will experience a greater level of energy, concentration and mental clarity every day. You will feel rejuvenated by your business day, ready to take on the rest of your life during your nonworking hours.

You can also build your feelings of self-mastery through mental rehearsal of success experiences. Athletes constantly rehearse successful performances in their minds prior to competition. The brain-booster routine (refer to Chapter 11) offers you a chance to mentally rehearse in this way. As you recall, the brain-booster phase of the resting-in-motion routine requires you to imagine going through your day full of energy and stamina, putting into practice all of the stamina secrets I have shared with you. Make sure you always include this technique in your routine. It will program your mental computer for confidence and success!

15

▼

A Six-Step Remedy for Executive Stress

The stamina attitude just described is an absolute necessity for successful stress management. It provides you with an outlook on life in which you are in charge and your life is well balanced between work, family, friends and your own personal world. Having this attitude can put stresses and strains in perspective. Once you recognize that work is only one part of your life rather than the *only* part, you'll be better able to take business stresses in stride.

In addition to the stamina attitude, you also must have a specific system to deal with day-to-day stress in the business world. It's the little irritations that occur daily—often the ones that you have the least control over—that are the most frustrating and energy-draining. How many times has one of these irritations happened to you lately?

- On your busiest day, someone in the office must see you *immediately* for a crucial discussion. Even though you're way behind with a top priority report, you agree to the meeting, only to discover that the ''crisis'' was a minimal problem that could—and should— have waited for another day.

- During a business trip to another city your taxi driver gets lost, making you 30 minutes late for an appointment with an important client.
- You discover that a year-end report you prepared and sent to the home office by express mail was lost en route.
- You give a small but important project to a seemingly bright and conscientious young associate only to find out that he misunderstood your instructions and now you must take on the project yourself and start all over.
- Your boss has an irritating habit of interrupting you whenever you're trying to present your ideas at management meetings.
- You spend several days developing a new marketing strategy for one of the company's new products, only to be told that top management is going to scrap the whole product line.
- After an exhausting day of business travel, you arrive at your hotel only to learn that they have no record of your reservation and are completely booked.
- Your children come down with the flu on a day when both you and your spouse are fully scheduled with appointments.
- You are getting dressed for work on a day when you need to look your best when the zipper on your favorite pants/skirt breaks.
- You fail to receive an important, prearranged transcontinental business telephone call at home because your teenage daughter was secretly on the bedroom phone for an hour talking to her boyfriend.

Stress: A Fact of Executive Life

These and other stresses, big and small, are all part of corporate life. There is absolutely no way to avoid them. Stress is not all bad, however. It can motivate, challenge and stimulate you. Many business managers actually thrive on stress. Too much stress can cause burn-out, but too little stress results in *rust-out*

If your life were completely stressless, day after day, you would soon stagnate. I'm sure that if you had wanted a completely calm existence your career choice would not have been the business world.

Let me tell you about Jeff, a successful corporate executive who, ironically, was under stress because he didn't have much stress in his life. Jeff is a 45-year-old self-made man who built a small computer parts company into a multimillion dollar venture. When he was building his company and on the way to the top he was certainly under a great deal of stress. He worked 12 to 14 hours a day; constantly fought deadlines for bids and orders; just barely avoided bankruptcy twice; and did much of the work with only a skeleton staff to support him. Now his company employs 120 people with a full complement of managers to run the company. Two years ago, he hired a chief operations officer and made himself the chief executive officer. He still made decisions about the company but, for the most part, the company ran on a day to day basis without him.

His main stress was that he had become obsolete. When he first came to me for help, Jeff expressed his dilemma this way:

> "I don't know what's wrong with me. I just don't get the same enjoyment out of my business that I used to. The challenge is gone. Business problems used to excite me and stir me to action. Now I know the business can—and does—run

pretty much without me. When I go into the assembly line area and start giving advice and direction like I did in the old days, the supervisors resent my usurping their authority. And even if they didn't resent it I still don't get the same kicks out of it. I'm just living my life from day to day. Some days I almost feel like a prisoner marking off the days of a long sentence on his cell wall. What's happened to me?''

I hear this familiar story from many successful executives. It may seem difficult to believe, but there are people out there who *need* stress to be happy.

Of course, I have seen a few rare people who, even though they are successful, prefer to function with little or no stress. I recall Craig, for example, who had made a killing in commercial real estate by the time he was 28 years old. He chose to retire and live off his interest. He did no work and let others handle his investments. His main stress in life was an annoyance at meeting new people and being asked the question, ''And what do *you* do?'' When he replied, ''Nothing,'' he was chided for his lack of initiative. ''A person your age should be working or else be bored to death,'' they would say. Finding perfect contentment with his life of ease, he came up with a new response to the ''What do you do?'' question that put an end to critiques of his lifestyle. ''Do?'' he would say. ''Do about what?''

Jeff's case is more typical than Craig's. He had reached a career plateau and was asking himself ''Now what?'' These plateaus can occur at any time in your career as an executive. Most of the time the business world just pulls you along into new ventures, so the slump doesn't last very long.

Actually, these plateaus in which the lack of stress is stressful are most pronounced in people whose work involves maximum creative effort. Take novelists, for example. They often put so much creative effort into writing that after a book is finished they experience a depressive episode. The depression is not so much related to a burnout from overwork as it is to that oddly disenchanted feeling that follows the attainment of important projects. It's a bit like feeling "Is that all there is to thin?" While there is joy over the accomplishment, a definite feeling of disappointment exists.

The reason for this slump is that the joy of working and the joy of living often lie more in the *striving* than in the accomplishing. The challenge, the hard work and even the enjoyment is in doing and trying and overcoming obstacles. Once you reach your goal—once you finish the report or are promoted to senior vice-president—you are pleased, of course, but perhaps not as pleased as you had expected.

The only way to get out of a slump such as this is to set new goals for yourself immediately. Actually, world-class executives avoid slumps because they think and plan far ahead: They set new goals for themselves and their companies all the time, so there is never a lag phase of letdown or inactivity.

This is exactly what Jeff needed to do. He actually had worked himself out of a job by being so successful. My suggestion was for him to work himself out even further by hiring a chief executive officer and making himself chairman of the board. This way, he was free to devote full energy to devising a new set of goals. Since he wasn't exactly sure what he wanted to do, his first goal was to concentrate on himself and his lack of energy by implementing the Hilton Head program.

Once he understood the basics of the program, Jeff forged ahead, gaining new stamina reserves and mental energy that allowed him to think through his business goals. After four months, he was setting up a plan of action for the establishment of a venture capital company which would enable him to invest in and help guide small business ventures. In this way, he would not be getting completely back into the old grind of setting up a new company, but he could take a role in the excitement and challenge of starting new companies from scratch.

You must monitor your personal and business goals so you are staying one step ahead. You must try not to accomplish even small goals in your business life without setting your sights on the next step in the process.

Managing Stress in Six Easy Steps

Even though a certain amount of stress is motivating and challenging, too much stress can also be extremely damaging. Since business stress is inevitable, your goal is to learn to cope with it and manage it, rather than eradicate it. You must manage stress just as you manage business matters.

Although the stress that affects your business life comes in every form, I have developed a six-step plan of action that you can use to help take business stress in stride and avoid its stamina-draining effects.

Whenever you experience business or family stress that is affecting your mental or physical stamina, go through the six-step procedure that follows.

Step 1: Examine Your Emotions

Before you try to figure out what is causing your stress and what you can do about it, take a few minutes to examine your emotions. You must determine how the stress is affecting you emotionally. Your first goal is to ask yourself, "Exactly what emotion am I feeling?"

In trying to solve any problem, the more details you have about what is going on the better. Some executives are experts at analyzing business issues, but are complete novices when it comes to figuring out their emotions.

Are you depressed, anxious, angry, bored, restless, irritated, jealous? It is important to determine *what* you are feeling because it may help to pinpoint the source of stress. Some emotions come in a disguised form. For example, while you may feel mild depression and listlessness, your true emotion may be one of anger as opposed to depression. Anger that is denied or unexpressed is often experienced as depression.

Let's suppose you are doing business with an executive from another company who is totally obnoxious. His ego is gigantic; his conversation is mostly about himself and how wonderful he is—just the kind of person you find intolerable. It is essential that your companies do business together, however. It is your job to convince him of this fact. Obviously, you're not going to tell him what a jerk he really is. You've had to meet with him, take him to lunch, and swallow your real feelings toward him. Under these circumstances, you may feel a combination of depression and frustration.

On the other hand, let's suppose the problem is with you rather than with the situation. Suppose that you and another manager are working on a project together; because you are more creative, the project is based almost totally on your ideas. After the project receives rave reviews from upper-level management, you discover that your co-worker is spreading the word that he did most of the work while you sloughed off. If you are the type of person who has trouble dealing with assertiveness and anger, you might suppress your feelings, convince yourself that what your co-worker did was really not that bad and experience a mild depression for several days. If situations like this continue and your response remains the same, you may develop a chronic depression and lack of stamina. The resolution of your stress lies in your coping with your *anger*, not your depression.

Many successful executives have the opposite problem: They become angry easily and are quick to vent their feelings, even with minor irritations. In such cases, the executive is usually acutely aware of his anger because it's very obvious. He may blame his stress, however, on the behavior of others rather than acknowledge his over-response to normal business frustrations.

Step 2. Defuse Your Emotions

If you are experiencing strong negative emotions because of stress, you must defuse some of this emotion before you can set out a plan of action. Keep in mind that alleviating some of the power of your emotional response to stress is only a temporary solution and only a first step in stress management.

Many executives try to defuse emotions through the use of food, alcohol or drugs. All of these further drain your energy reserves that you so desperately need to help you cope with the stress. Moreover, their effects are short-term and, for the most part, ineffectual. If you are under the care of a physician, however, who prescribes and supervises a regimen of medication for your emotions, by all means, keep your treatment plan going. Just don't experiment on your own or use food or alcohol as tranquilizers.

There are three basic ways to defuse stress-induced emotions:

1. The resting-in-motion routine
2. The Hilton Head stamina fitness plan
3. The talking-it-out strategy

The first two techniques have been described in earlier chapters as ways to increase stamina and enhance overall health. They also serve to reduce stress, however. As I mentioned earlier, both resting-in-motion and the stamina fitness plan relax you better than meditation and actually help your brain fight negative emotions associated with stress. By practicing these routines regularly, you are actually strengthening your mind and body so that when stress comes along you automatically cope more effectively. The movement and exercise part of these plans helps you work out emotions such as anxiety, depression and anger.

If you've had a particularly stressful day, you can defuse your emotion by an extra resting-in-motion routine or by doing a little extra of my stamina fitness plan described in detail in Chapter 10.

My talking-it-out strategy is relatively simple but effective in defusing emotion. Talking about your feelings to a receptive, supportive person can make a big difference in how you feel. To be realistic, not everybody is interested in listening to your feelings. And you may not want to confide in business associates for fear that your emotional openness may be interpreted as a sign of weakness and be used against you in the future.

You must choose a person who will want to listen, who will respect the confidential nature of your conversation and who will not ridicule you—no matter what your feelings. Ideally, they should *not* be associated with your business life. Obviously, this should be a person who cares about you and your feelings. Typical candidates for this role are a spouse, close relative or close friend. If none of these is available and your stress is severe enough to interfere continually with your normal functioning in life, then a professional such as a psychologist, psychiatrist, social worker or other health service provider trained in stress management should be consulted.

Talking to this person about how you feel won't solve your problem, but it will defuse your emotion, clear out your mind and make you feel better. Clearing out mental clutter is the first step in coping with stress.

You must choose a confidant who will be a good listener and who will be emotionally supportive. At this stage in the stress management process, *you are not seeking advice or possible solutions to your stress problem*, because your goal now is to defuse emotion, not to look for solutions.

Let's suppose you were very upset with a subordinate for not handling a client as you would have. You are angry even though the deal went through and everything turned out okay. You start expressing your feelings of frustration to your closest friend when he says, "Well, I don't know what you're so upset about. Just tell him off or forget it." Now what your friend just did was to put the cork back in your emotional bottle just when you were trying to release your stressful emotions. Whether his advice is any good or not is beside the point. What you need him to do is to listen and say something such as "I bet that made you really angry. I know how upset you must be. Tell me more."

Your friend doesn't have to be your therapist; he or she just has to listen and be supportive. Advice and simple solutions will stop the defusing process and probably make you feel worse.

Make sure you choose someone to talk to who is likely to give you the right response. Later on you will need a problem solver, but now you need a *listener*. Some people are actually good at both. They know when to advise and when to shut up and listen. Or you may have one person you go to for listening and support and another for practical advice. In fact, the supportive person may have little practical sense when it comes to solutions and the practical advisor may have little patience or understanding as far as emotions are concerned.

Step 3: Pinpoint the Reasons for Your Stress

Sometimes the cause of your stress is obvious. You are angry at a fellow manager or subordinate. You are depressed because your department just lost a big account. You are anxious because your company was just bought out by a conglomerate and you're worried about your future with the company. You are frustrated because office politics is making it more difficult for you to get the promotion you deserve.

If you are not exactly sure where the stress is coming from, divide your life into past, present and future. Begin by looking in the recent past for stressful events. Examine your appointment calendar for the past week. Go through your business, family and social life for the last few days. If you really think about it, there may have been an event or series of events that upset you more than you realize.

Next, look at your present situation. What is happening today? Any likely sources of stress? Then project yourself into the future. Are you worrying about a future meeting? Are you simply worried about the future in general? What about concerns at home? Your children? Your spouse?

Sometimes stress is ongoing rather than in any one time period: It may be a way of life you are stressed about. It may be a long-term dissatisfaction with your job, your spouse or something about yourself.

If you can't determine what is stressing you, ask your spouse or a friend for their analysis. If the stress continues without your being able to determine the cause, you may want to consult a professional.

Step 4: Determine What Kind of Action Is Possible

Now ask yourself "Is there anything I can do to change the circumstances that are causing me stress?" If your answer is "No," then go on to Step 5.

If your answer is "Yes," your next goal is to develop a plan of action to confront the problem and implement that plan. If you need advice or assistance with your plan, search for it. Ask a friend or your spouse how they would handle the situation. Once you take action you may solve the cause of your stress and no more steps in the stress-management process will be necessary.

With some stresses, you may feel that a particular action could change the problem but, for your own reasons, you choose not to take that action. For example, you may experience stress because of your marriage, your job or where you live. Now you could get a divorce, change careers or move to another city. Or, more than likely, you may say "I could do these things but I'm not going to." You may not choose these actions because you may feel that while your career is bad it may not be *that* bad. Perhaps it isn't feasible to relocate to another city. Or you may be uncertain about the future. Change, even for the better, is scary. You might make a major change in your life and end up worse than you were before.

Since most decisions about stressful events are not clear-cut, all of us end up being indecisive at times. Unfortunately, indecision can go on for days, weeks, even years. In the long run, chronic indecision about a stress can be stressful in and of itself. After you have carefully weighed all of the alternatives, force yourself to make a decision. Even deciding that there is nothing you can do about the stressful situation is a decision.

Step 5: Get Your Thoughts Out of Your Head

If this is a stress that you can't do anything about or if you have taken action but you still feel upset, your solution lies in your head. We all talk to ourselves in our minds. You are probably only partially aware of what you are thinking most of the time, but certainly your thoughts have a major bearing on your feelings.

When we are stressed we tend to fall into very irrational and illogical thinking that works against us. This "stress thinking" actually keeps you trapped in negative emotions. Because of this, you must identify what you are saying to yourself about your stress so you can begin to change your thought patterns. You are most likely making certain assumptions and interpretations about your stress that are not logical. Therefore, you continue to remain upset.

In order to identify and change your thinking patterns, you must first dispel your thoughts about the stressful circumstances. Simply take out a piece of paper and write down exactly what you are thinking about your stress. Do not try to interpret your thoughts at this point, simply act like a recording secretary and write down each thought as you think it. Some people prefer to talk their thoughts out into a tape recorder because they feel they get a more accurate picture of what they are saying to themselves. The first time you actually hear your stress thoughts played back to you, it's a little shocking. Most people react by saying, "No wonder I feel so upset. Listen to what I'm saying to myself!"

Let me give you an example of what such a "stress list" looks like by using the case of Margaret. Margaret is a 35-year-old bank manager who is married to an orthopedic surgeon. They are both very busy, highly successful people. In the course of her total health evaluation at the Hilton Head Health Institute, it became evident that her lack of stamina was, at least in part, due to her inability to cope with stress. During her stay in my program, we discussed a recent stressful event at her bank that still made her anxious a month after it happened. Apparently, Margaret had recommended Sheila, a friend of hers, to take over the position as chief of loan operations. This was an important position within the bank and Margaret wanted to recommend the right person for the job. The candidates were narrowed down to two and on Margaret's recommendation Sheila was hired.

Sheila took over the position with enthusiasm and was extremely efficient. Six months later, however, unbeknownst to Margaret, Sheila developed family problems and began to drink to excess. Apparently, Sheila had given up alcohol several years before because of a drinking problem. At first Sheila was shrewd enough to keep her drinking a secret, but it slowly took its toll on her efficiency at work.

Three months later Margaret discovered that Sheila had been falsifying her monthly loan reports to cover up questionable loans she had approved. She also had been arriving for work late, leaving early and taking an excessive number of sick days. Sheila was fired and the bank scrambled to offset losses on the bad loans. Luckily, the losses were minimal.

Obviously, Margaret was extremely upset by the incident, since she had recommended Sheila. She was especially apprehensive about how the turn of events would affect her career with the bank, even though she was the one who discovered the erroneous reports and had taken immediate action. In fact, her quick actions had probably saved the bank thousands of dollars.

Since this stress happened a month earlier and was still causing Margaret anxiety I asked her to put her thoughts about the stress on a piece of paper. Her list of thoughts is reproduced below:

- This is a catastrophe.
- This is probably the worst thing that has ever happened to me.
- This probably means the bank will never trust my judgment again.
- Maybe they think I'm incompetent or that my reports are inaccurate too.

- I'm a failure in my career.
- I can't do anything right and nothing ever goes my way.
- My business life is over.

Thoughts such as these have an enormous influence over emotions. This type of thinking will continue Margaret's stress reaction, and unless these thought patterns are modified she will continue to feel anxious and depressed. In turn, her work performance will certainly suffer.

Step 6: Reprogram Your Mental Computer

Now that you have listed your stress-related thinking patterns, it is time to reprogram the computer in your mind. Examine your thought patterns and ask yourself the following questions:

1. Am I exaggerating the scope and importance of the stressful situation?

When under stress, you have a tendency to see problems out of proportion. Small stresses seem big and big stresses appear catastrophic. A few days or weeks later you'll probably ask yourself, "Why did I get so upset about something so insignificant?"

Put the stress in proper perspective by considering how important it is in relation to all the *possible* problems that you could have. It may be that you are too close to your own life and problems. Ask yourself, "How important is this stress compared to the worldwide problems of mankind? Where does my stress fit into the universe, from the beginning to the end of time?"

How terrible is it that you are late for a manager's meeting compared to all the possible tragedies in the world?

Don't get me wrong, I don't want you to be apathetic and irresponsible about your work, I just want you to back off from your own personal world and view individual stressful circumstances in their proper perspective.

2. Am I guilty of all-or-nothing thinking?

Stress blocks your mind in such a way that your interpretations of events become more rigid. You tend to see things in extreme categories: Circumstances are either right or wrong, good or bad, fair or unfair, with no gradations between.

As an example, let's say you are an overweight executive trying to lose a few pounds. After an especially tiring day, your sugar cravings get the best of you and you down a pint of chocolate ice cream. Now you're stressed and guilt-ridden over the lapse in your resolve. Your conversation with yourself goes something like this: "Well, I blew it again. I'm off my diet. I knew I couldn't last for very long. I keep losing my willpower."

Clearly you see yourself as being in one of two categories—a dieter or a nondieter. One slip—even one cookie—and you are no longer dieting. Obviously, when you are "on" your diet you perceive yourself as a good, honest and strong-willed person. When you are "off" the diet you are likely to become quite a different character: "I've been bad. I cheated. I wish I had willpower like other people." In the wink of an eye, you go from Dr. Jekyll to Mr. Hyde.

You must force yourself to think of stresses *along a continuum*. If, while dieting, you overeat, then you have simply eaten too much. You have not "gone off your diet." You just slipped a little. You are not a different person, so there should not be any change in your basic self-esteem.

Challenge all-or-nothing thinking and don't let yourself get away with it.

3. Am I overgeneralizing?

Some of your thoughts may indicate that you are drawing a sweeping conclusion based on a single incident. Thoughts such as "I failed, therefore, I am a complete failure" or "I didn't get that assignment, therefore, I *never* get what I want" are classic examples of overgeneralization.

Such illogical reasoning only keeps you upset. You must question this type of reasoning and search for ways to disprove such conclusions. Review all of the times when you did *not* fail and all of the times when you *did* get what you wanted.

Remind yourself that even the most successful executives fail every once in a while. In fact, successful people have usually tasted defeat more than most. Og Mandino, the motivational writer and speaker, makes this point by reminding us that even though Hank Aaron hit 755 career home runs, he also struck out more than 1200 times!

One method of avoiding these irrational overgeneralizations about yourself is to make certain that your self-esteem is based on stable, unchanging traits that are impervious to day-to-day happenings. Your basic self-esteem might be based on the premise that you are a successful, intelligent, creative and caring person. You must firmly believe that these qualities are deeply rooted and unchangeable, even if you occasionally fail, act stupidly, are unimaginative or are insensitive to others. These episodes prove that you are subject to human frailties, not that you are a despicable character. Unless you start basing your conception of who you really are on these solid personal qualities, your emotions will bounce up and down, fluctuating with the natural good and bad that happens to all of us in our lives.

4. Am I jumping to conclusions?

Do any of your thoughts indicate that you are coming to a conclusion or are forming an opinion based on insufficient evidence or, perhaps, on no evidence at all? Are you telling yourself that the boss is displeased with your work simply because he failed to say hello to you this morning? Or, perhaps, that a subordinate is a poor manager because he has difficulty speaking in front of large groups?

You must challenge the evidence for your conclusions and question your logic. Is there enough evidence? Is there *any* evidence? If not, change your conclusion or erase it completely.

5. Are my expectations too high?

Many executives, even successful ones, set goals for themselves and others that are unrealistic. For example, your stress-related thought may be: "Sophia should be handling that account exactly as I would." When you analyze this statement you realize that Sophia is managing the account extremely well, even though she is doing it quite differently than you would do it.

Therefore, there is no real reason for her to be handling it the same way you do—other than your assumption that the world would be better off if things were always done the way you do them.

Perhaps your expectations of yourself and your own performance are also too high. Are you being too idealistic? Are you thinking, "I closed that crucial deal well, after a lot of hard work. But maybe I could have done a better job, maybe I should have put even more time into it."

Of course, you should try your best, but once you've put your best into it, forget it. You must allow yourself to feel joy in your accomplishments.

Once you have analyzed and challenged your thought patterns in this way, you are ready to reprogram your mental computer. Based on the challenges you just made to your faulty thinking patterns, you can now devise new, more productive ways of thinking about the same stressful event.

First, write these new thoughts on a piece of paper. Then, in a firm and purposeful voice, record them on a tape recorder.

To give you a more concrete example, let's go back to Margaret's stress-related thoughts regarding the episode in which her friend was fired from the bank after falsifying reports. Look back a few pages and review the faulty thinking patterns that were worsening Margaret's anxiety and frustration. Now read the new thoughts that she recorded to counteract her stress problem:

- This is certainly an upsetting situation, but it is *not* anything I can't handle.
- It's bad, but things could have been a lot worse. I caught her before our losses became astronomical.
- The top-level bank executives were probably furious when they found out, but I'm sure they've gotten over it by now.
- Just because I recommended a person who turned out to have problems doesn't mean that I am not trustworthy or that my judgment is poor.
- Things like this may happen to me again, but most of the time I am in control of myself and my work. Besides, I've had a lot of fortunate breaks in my career with the bank.
- My career is still strong and I can profit from this experience. Dealing effectively with the stress created by this crisis will strengthen me for future bad times.
- Even if the bank decides to take it out on me, I am a competent business professional who has a lot to offer any organization.

When you have tape-recorded your thoughts, play them back and listen to them carefully. Listen and *learn*. It may take you a short while to reprogram your mind, so pay close attention even if you don't completely agree with what you are hearing. Don't argue with the new thoughts. Accept them as new data for your mental computer.

Listen to these tape-recorded thoughts twice a day for the next 10 days. Always pay close attention. Your mind must be clear while you are doing this and you should not have any distractions.

The power of this remedy is amazing. Before you know it, your old thoughts will be replaced by the new ones. If you hear one of the old thoughts during the day, replace it immediately with one of the new ones. Or better yet, play the tape for yourself.

As you continue to deal with stress in this way you'll find it becomes easier and easier. In fact, your mind will automatically begin to question and confront illogical and irrational stress-related thinking without your conscious effort.

You'll slowly become a better stress manager, resulting in better control of your emotional reactions and dramatically increasing your energy and stamina.

16

▼

Special
Stamina Needs
of Women Executives

While the Hilton Head program has proven its effectiveness with both men and women executives, women managers face special stamina problems that slightly alter my regimen for them. Of the executives who participate in our program on Hilton Head Island, 50% are women. More women are entering the executive world daily and more are working their way up to the top levels of corporations. Since 1980 more than 25% of all candidates for MBA degrees in the top 10 business schools in the country have been women.

Women executives who participate in my program tend to be relatively young, between the ages of 25 and 40. The men, however, are older, usually ranging in age from 40 to 60. In analyzing this age differential, I found that women managers are more likely to recognize personal needs, admit to those needs and seek professional help to overcome their problems. Their male counterparts tend to be less willing to admit to the need for help. Unfortunately, it often takes high blood pressure, high cholesterol, diabetes or even a heart attack before a male executive will seek help. I've known some men to put up with chronic fatigue and lack of stamina for years, allowing these problems to seriously interfere with managerial performance, rather than admit that anything was wrong. Perhaps because they feel the draining effect of demands on both the work and homefront more acutely than many men, women managers learn early in their careers to take care of their most valuable business asset—themselves.

In addition to the executive stamina problems that I have already discussed in this book, women managers must concern themselves with their stamina in relation to special nutritional needs, pregnancy, menstruation and menopause, as well as career stress. What follows are suggestions for coping successfully with these issues, and using the Hilton Head program to remove the special barriers to energy experienced by many women executives.

The Special Nutritional Needs of Women

Calcium

The results of recent studies have caused many health professionals to advocate raising the *calcium* requirement for women by about 50%. The concern is over changes in calcium metabolism with age that can result in a thinning of your bones called *osteoporosis*, which increases the risks of fractures and compression of the spine. There may be as many as 20 million post-menopausal American women suffering from osteoporosis. Many experts agree that the time to start calcium supplements is when you are around 35 years of age. This is when some women begin to show a negative balance of calcium. Other experts, however, have questioned the usefulness of calcium supplements after this age, since they feel that more research is needed on the complex nature of osteoporosis before prevention strategies are recommended. You can increase your intake of milk, cheese, soybeans and leafy green vegetables, but you still may not satisfy your nutritional needs for calcium. Besides, you may end up going overboard with protein intake (or with fat, in the case of consuming more dairy products). High protein intake—above the 15% of your daily calories that I have recommended—can reduce the amount of calcium absorbed. This is the last thing you want to have happen!

Prior to menopause, women may need up to 1000 mg to 1200 mg of calcium each day. Postmenopausal women may need up to 1500 mg unless they are undergoing estrogen therapy to slow bone loss, in which case they may need only 1000 mg.

I suggest you find a calcium supplement that has between 250 mg and 500 mg of calcium per tablet so you won't have to take a lot of pills every day. Since you will probably get about 500 mg of calcium from the foods that you eat, two 250-mg tablets of calcium per day should be sufficient if you are premenopausal. Postmenopausal women should take two 500-mg tablets of calcium per day. Your body uses calcium most efficiently if you spread the dose out, taking one supplement in the morning and one in the evening.

You should consult your physician before taking calcium supplements. Moreover, there is some evidence to show that excess calcium may increase your risk of kidney stones if you have had kidney stones or have a family history of them, so be sure to consult your physician if this applies to you.

There are many over-the-counter calcium supplements on the market containing various forms of calcium. For example, you may see any one of the following types of calcium in supplements: calcium carbonate, calcium lactate, calcium gluconate, bone meal and dolomite. Probably the best supplement is calcium carbonate because it contains the highest concentration of calcium, is relatively inexpensive and is free of toxins. Such supplements as bone meal and dolomite may be contaminated with lead or mercury.

You may also wish to increase your calcium consumption by taking in more calcium through your diet. Any of the following provide approximately 300 mg of calcium:

- 1 cup skim or low-fat milk
- 1 cup plain yogurt
- 1½ oz Cheddar cheese
- 3 oz sardines, with bones
- 1½ cups spinach
- 1 cup collard greens

Iron

Women who experience long menstrual cycles or heavy blood losses during menstruation may have a problem with iron deficiency. Tufts University reports that women between the ages of 12 and 50 years consume only about 60% of their iron needs per day. Since iron helps to release oxygen to body cells for energy production, iron deficiency can result in fatigue, irritability and headaches.

Prior to menopause, women need 18 mg of iron per day. These premenopausal woman lose about 1.5 mg of iron a day, but can store only 300 mg or less. Men, on the other hand, lose only 1 mg of iron per day but can store up to 1000 mg of iron in their bone marrow, liver, and spleen. The iron needs of men and of postmenopausal women are 10 mg per day, about half that of younger women.

Some foods rich in iron are the following:

Food (3½ oz portion)	Iron Content
Oysters	6.5 mg
Dried apricots	4.5 mg
Clams	3.0 mg
Whole wheat, Pumpernickel, enriched white bread	3.0 mg
Lean beef	2.5 mg
Raisins	2.0 mg
Tofu	2.0 mg
Tuna	1.5 mg
Chicken	1.0 mg

If you are eating a variety of these foods each day, you probably don't have anything to worry about in terms of your daily iron allowance. If not, you may choose to use a commercial iron supplement of 30 mg per day just to be sure. Consult your physician about this since, if you suffer from chronic lack of energy, there may be other reasons for it—such as anemia.

Although it is almost impossible to consume too much iron from your normal daily intake of food, *overdosing with iron supplements can be toxic*. Most experts agree that total daily iron intake ranging from 25 to 75 mg is safe. Some people could probably get away with higher doses with no ill effects, but such doses are ill-advised because of the possibility of hemochromatosis. This is a genetic disease that causes damage to your heart, pancreas, and liver due to accumulations of iron in these organs. While only about 1 in

1000 people has this disease, 1 in 10 people carries one of the two genes necessary for the disease to occur and, therefore, may be susceptible to iron overdosing.

Overdoses of iron can be particularly toxic in children. Iron pills or vitamin/mineral supplements containing iron should be kept in child-resistant bottles well out of the reach of your children.

Total Calorie Intake

While women should be eating the same proportions of protein, carbohydrate and fat as men (following the guidelines in Chapters 5, 6 and 7), they should not be eating as many total calories each day as men. Women burn, on the average, about 500 fewer calories per day than men. One reason for this in some cases is the fact that men tend to have more body mass (a multiple of your height and weight) and muscle tissue than women. Body mass is a factor in metabolism simply because it takes more energy to run a big machine than a small one.

The prime reason for metabolic differences between the sexes, however, has to do with muscle tissue. Ideally, a man's body contains only about 15% to 20% fat, leaving him with an abundance of lean body mass. Women have more fat—about 20% to 25%—and, therefore, relatively less muscle. (These are ideal fat percentages. Many of the women who attend our program have, as the result of our initial evaluation, anywhere from 25% to 50% fat with very little muscle tone due to physical inactivity.)

Muscle is metabolically much more active than fat tissue. Even inactive muscle burns more energy (i.e., calories) than fat. Therefore, there is a correlation between the amount of muscle tissue in your body and your basal metabolic rate. Simply stated, the more muscle and the less fat you have, the more you can eat.

In order to maximize your body's use of the calories you eat each day, just follow the fitness plan outlined in Chapter 9. It is designed to help you burn off fat *and* increase muscle tissue. While it would be extremely difficult to completely close the gender gap in this regard, if you build up muscle tissue you will be able to increase your calorie intake each day by at least 100 to 200 calories without gaining weight.

Age is also a factor affecting metabolism in both women and men. As you age, you may be less physically active. Also, through the aging process you tend to lose lean body mass even if you do exercise (although not as much as if you were sedentary).

The following gives you an idea of exactly how much a 125-pound adult woman with an average level of physical activity (e.g., either one hour of walking per day with a sedentary desk job, or minimal exercise with a job that requires a great deal of walking and moving around) could eat each day throughout her lifetime.

Daily Caloric Needs of a 125-lb Woman

Age	Calories
20	2000
30	1900
40	1800
50	1700
60	1700
70	1500
80	1500

By eating the number of calories indicated for your age and by following the Hilton Head Stamina Fitness program, you will be able to maintain a stable weight.

The Pregnant Executive

Nutrition

If you are pregnant, your nutrition must change slightly if you are to stay healthy and energetic. In all matters concerning pregnancy, you should let your obstetrician be your guide. What follows are general nutritional guidelines; your personal needs may be different. In addition, *never begin a vitamin/mineral supplement regimen during pregnancy without the advice of your physician*.

When you are pregnant, three special changes occur with regard to your nutritional needs:

- You need more food calories.

A pregnant woman should eat about 15% more calories per day during the first trimester of her pregnancy. In most cases this would mean an extra 150 calories per day. During the final six months this should be increased to an extra 350 calories per day. Weight gain, of course, is normal during pregnancy, with 20 to 30 pounds being acceptable in most cases. It is *not* a good idea to diet during pregnancy, since you will not be getting the extra nutrients your body needs by reducing calories. Moreover, dieting during pregnancy has been linked to low birth weight in babies. If you are gaining too much weight or are not sure which foods to eat, let your physician advise you.

- You need more protein.

Your need for protein increases from 45 gms per day to 75 gms a day. Since there are 4 calories in one gram of protein, you should be eating about 300 or more calories of protein-rich food per day. This need could be met by eating two to three ounces of poultry, fish, cheese or meat three to four times a day. If you are a vegetarian, 1 to 1½ cups of cooked dried beans, peas or lentils three times a day would supply this need.

- You need an increased amount of some vitamins and minerals.

The following is a list of the recommended dietary allowances (RDA) of vitamins and minerals that should be increased during pregnancy.

	Not Pregnant	*Pregnant*
Vitamin A	4000 IU	5000 IU
Vitamin C	60 mg	80 mg
Vitamin D	400 IU	400 IU
Vitamin E	8 mg	10 mg
Thiamin	1 mg	1.4 mg
Riboflavin	1.2 mg	1.5 mg
Niacin	13 mg	15 mg
Vitamin B_6	2.0 mg	2.6 mg
Folic acid	0.4 mg	0.8 mg
Vitamin B_{12}	3 mcg (micrograms)	4 mcg (micrograms)
Calcium	1000 to 1200 mg	1500 mg
Phosphorus	800 mg	1200 mg
Magnesium	300 mg	450 mg
Iron	18 mg	50 mg
Zinc	15 mg	20 mg
Iodine	150 mg	175 mg

Of this entire list your greatest need is for more iron, folic acid and calcium. Most obstetricians recommend a 30- to

60-mg supplement of iron during pregnancy. Increased folic acid requirements can be met by eating 1 or 2 cups of any of the following each day:

> Spinach
> Turnip greens
> Endive
> Okra
> Broccoli
> Cauliflower
> Peas
> Romaine lettuce
> Liver
> Wheat germ

Calcium can be increased by following my supplementation guidelines for calcium described earlier in this chapter.

Physical Activity

Exercise is as important during pregnancy as at any other time in a woman's life. Unless your physician has specific restrictions for you, there is no reason you cannot continue to follow the fitness plan outlined in Chapter 10 during your pregnancy. In fact, if practiced carefully and correctly, it will help keep your stamina level high, keep you flexible and strengthen muscles in your abdomen and lower back, providing extra support for your growing baby.

The American College of Obstetricians and Gynecologists recommends walking, swimming and cycling for pregnant women as long as their pulse rate during exercise does not exceed 140 beats a minute for more than 15 minutes. Thus, you may have to modify the target heart rate that you used when you were not pregnant for my stamina stride (refer to Chapter 10) and be more leisurely with your walking.

Of course, you should always consult your obstetrician about any exercise during pregnancy.

Morning Sickness

Morning sickness is a normal although unpleasant aspect of pregnancy that may interfere with your work efficiency and stamina during any part of your workday, since nausea from pregnancy is not limited to the morning hours. Fortunately, in most cases, such nausea lasts only for the first trimester.

The nausea is caused by a slowing down of your digestive processes in early pregnancy, causing your food to remain in your stomach longer than usual. Actually, the best treatment for this sickness is to eat four to five smaller meals a day and to avoid greasy, fatty or rich foods—just what the Hilton Head Stamina Nutritional Plan calls for! Most women report that a little dry toast or crackers alleviate these feelings. You might try keeping some crackers at the office or in your briefcase in case of an emergency.

Premenstrual Syndrome and Menstruation

The physical and psychological aspects of premenstrual syndrome (PMS) and the menstrual cycle regularly contribute to a loss of energy and stamina in many women executives. Although the energy drain is a cyclical rather than a constant influence, energy may be affected as much as a week to two weeks a month, especially for those who suffer from premenstrual difficulties.

Premenstrual syndrome is a complex condition prior to menstruation characterized by water retention, muscle tension, depression, irritability, exhaustion, headaches, tender breasts, food cravings, backaches and joint pains. It is complex primarily because it is not as yet completely understood. Although exact figures are not known, as many as 33% of women under age 50 may suffer from this syndrome.

Popular treatments include high complex-carbohydrate diets, progesterone therapy, vitamin B_6 (pyridoxine) supplements, primrose oil, vitamin E supplements, and reductions in caffeine, salt, alcohol, sugar, fat and even calcium. The scientific support for these treatments is very scanty and any treatments along these lines must at the present time be considered experimental. Primrose oil, for example, is thought by some to increase body chemicals known as prostaglandins which in turn may alter hormone levels, thereby alleviating PMS symptoms. No substantial evidence for this claim exists, however.

Based on what I have said in earlier chapters on the dangers of vitamin/mineral overdoses, you should be wary of any treatment advocating high doses of vitamin B_6. Remember, severe neurological disturbances can occur with regular doses of 200 mg or more per day. What is most frightening is that I have been consulted by women executives who have been advised to take as much as 600 mg of vitamin B_6 each day for PMS relief!

The worst advice often given to women with premenstrual syndrome is to reduce calcium intake. This treatment is shocking, since women should actually be supplementing calcium because of the dangers of osteoporosis.

Women often report at least some relief from the following dietary changes:

- Increase in complex-carbohydrate consumption
- Decrease in salt consumption
- Decrease in alcohol, fat and sugar

All of these recommendations are in exact agreement with the Hilton Head stamina nutrition plan. I believe this plan is at least partially effective in combating PMS because it is designed to energize the body, reduce food cravings and reduce fluid retention. I have found over and over again that the participants who attend our Institute rarely experience strong food cravings while following the eating plans, since these plans are high in complex carbohydrates and low in sugar.

The stamina fitness plan also may help both the difficulties of premenstrual tension and the fatigue of the menstrual cycle itself. Its moderate but comprehensive design is usually associated with a definite decrease in menstrual discomfort. Women executives suffering from PMS report less fatigue, depression and food cravings after instituting this fitness plan.

As a woman executive, you can implement the diet and fitness program outlined in this book with confidence that not only will it provide extra stamina, but it will also work on your behalf when there is an extra drain on your system as the result of menstruation.

Coping with the Stress of Being a Woman Executive

Many women executives must deal with types of work stress that are specific to their gender. To give you a better idea of what I am referring to, let's examine the case of Phyllis.

Phyllis is a real success story in the corporate world. Coming from a hard-working but poor family, Phyllis studied hard as a youngster and earned scholarships through school. At the age of 23, she received her MBA from a prestigious business school on the east coast. She was hired by a large brokerage firm in New York, and over the next 10 years she became one of the leading financial analysts on Wall Street. During her rise to the top, Phyllis married Bob, a tax attorney, and gave birth to two children, Melissa and Edward.

When Phyllis came to my program she was 34 years old and her children were aged 2 and 4. Here is how Phyllis described her problem:

"Over the past few months I've had very little energy. I'm still productive at work, but it seems to be taking more effort than it used to. With my job, husband, children and friends, it takes most of my energy just to keep myself doing the minimum from day to day. I know I don't take care of myself as I should. I rarely exercise and I'm worried about my eating binges. I don't want to burn myself out just when I've reached a level of achievement in my career and just when I've started a family."

After my staff and I evaluated Phyllis' medical, nutritional, fitness and stress status, we targeted the following problems for change:

1. Phyllis had erratic eating habits which were responsible for a drain on her energy level. She never ate breakfast, she drank eight to ten cups of coffee per day, and she ate an abundance of high-sugar foods particularly late at night.

2. She rarely exercised, primarily because she felt she did not have the time. Occasionally she went to an aerobics class with a friend, but because of the travel time to and from the health club, she could not fit exercise into her daily schedule. Of course, since she exercised so infrequently, the class was strenuous and unpleasant for her, and she had no incentive to continue.

3. Within the past three months, Phyllis had gotten into the habit of staying up until 2 or 3 a.m. She had difficulty winding down from her day and couldn't fall asleep until very late. She referred to these late night hours, after her husband and children were asleep, as *her* time. She felt free during these hours because she was able to do whatever she

pleased, but this was when she overindulged in sweets.

4. Phyllis was experiencing stress at work over the past few weeks. Her workload was increasing and she was understaffed. The other analysts had three or four assistants, while she had only two. She had not brought this up to her boss for fear of being seen as a complainer who was not capable of handling her job. Since she was one of the few women to rise to her level within the company, it was important to Phyllis to *prove* that she could compete successfully with her male counterparts by doing more work than any of them. In addition, one of her male assistants was very uneasy about having a woman in authority over him; he followed her instructions begrudgingly. She had tried several approaches to no avail, finally realizing that his basic insecurity and defensiveness were not going to change.

5. Phyllis felt she had very little time for herself. Although she and her husband shared the household chores, there was just too much parenting and housework for both of them to handle along with their busy careers.

These fatigue factors in Phyllis's life illustrate many of the concerns of women executives. The time constraints of running a successful career and taking care of family responsibilities left Phyllis little time for herself. The treadmill she was on resulted in poor eating and exercise habits, the result of which only compounded her fatigue and reduced her fitness level. Although her husband helped with the cleaning, family bookkeeping and parenting, his business hours were longer than hers, leaving her to cook dinner, feed the children and prepare them for bed. This left her with the sole parenting role in the early evening when the children's demands for attention were the greatest (since they had not seen either parent all day) and when she was at her lowest point both physically and emotionally.

A recent Boston University study of working couples revealed that the combination of work and family responsibilities puts more stress on women than on men. Of the 651 male and female employees surveyed, the married women spent up to 85 hours a week working at the office and at home. Obviously, that's two full-time jobs. While the study also found that the men shared in the household chores, they spent about 20 hours less in combined office/home work than women. When children were sick, working women were more likely to stay home than their working spouses by a margin of 6 to 1.

My staff and I set up a plan of action for Phyllis that was designed to attack each of her five major problem areas. Of the six factors that cause executive fatigue (described in Chapter 3), Phyllis was obviously suffering from three of them: nutrient fatigue, dehydration fatigue and stress fatigue. Here's how we helped Phyllis begin her new stamina lifestyle.

Problem 1—Inadequate Nutrition

Plan of Action:

I started Phyllis immediately on the Hilton Head stamina nutrition plan. For her, this meant breakfast every morning and a more balanced, high complex-carbohydrate, low-fat, low-sodium, high-fiber diet.

She was restricted to two cups of caffeinated coffee per day, one in the early morning and the other after her evening meal (unless she had business to attend to after dinner). All caffeinated soft drinks were also eliminated. Her high caffeine intake during the day was taking a toll on her energy, with the result that she was draining her system of fluid all day long. She was instructed to consume my stamina drink—8 ounces of orange juice mixed with 4 ounces of carbonated water (see Chapter 12)—three times a day: in the morning, afternoon and evening. Decaffeinated coffee, tea and diet soft drinks were additional options.

Her high sugar intake particularly late in the evening, while giving her a temporary lift, was leading to slumps in her blood sugar level, causing more fatigue and lethargy. It also resulted in an extra 15 pounds of weight that not only put an extra burden on her body, but also made her feel frumpy and unattractive. This is why I started her out on the weight-control option of my nutrition plan and then switched her to the female maintenance plan after she had lost her weight (this took about 5 weeks).

The high complex-carbohydrate intake on the food plans helped to control some of her sugar cravings. During the first week of her new eating pattern, a snack of a piece of fruit at about 10:00 p.m. helped stave her hunger. After the first few days on the meal plan, the majority of her sugar cravings were over; when she does have a food craving it is much less severe and easier to overcome.

Problem 2—Inadequate Exercise

Plan of Action:

To help her lose weight and increase energy reserves, I also started Phyllis on our fitness plan, scheduling four days of stamina striding alternating with three days of stamina strengthening exercises. She chose to do these exercises first thing in the morning. She and her husband bought a treadmill so she could continue her walking program even in inclement weather.

To provide uninterrupted time for her morning exercises, Phyllis arranged with her husband that he be in charge of preparing breakfast, taking care of the children and completing any necessary household chores each morning prior to the arrival of their babysitter/housekeeper. This seemed only fair since he worked late more often than she did, leaving her with the dinner preparations and early evening chores on most nights. In fact, Bob, her husband, subsequently tried to arrange his schedule so that he could go to work a little later than usual each morning.

This schedule worked well for Phyllis, since she preferred to do her exercising at home rather than at a health club. She felt she could go at her own pace and she also enjoyed the solitude provided by her exercise time. A rule was established in the household that, no matter what, she was not to be bothered during her exercise time. This was easier said than done in the beginning, especially with two small children. With the assistance of Bob, however, she was left completely alone 95% of the time.

In addition to following our stamina fitness plan, Phyllis was advised to schedule a resting-in-motion routine each afternoon. Because of the demands made of her as soon as she returned home each evening, she decided to schedule resting-in-motion late in her workday at the office. At the end of her day she would hold all calls, close her office door and leisurely complete the routine, topping it off with a power snack of an orange and a Perrier. This served as her transition time between work and home and energized her both physically and emotionally for the next two to three hours when she needed stamina for her role as mother and wife.

Problem 3—Inadequate Sleep

Plan of Action:

Staying up late and getting up early had begun to take its toll on Phyllis. Sleep/wake schedules are habits, just like any others, that can become very strongly entrenched once they are established. Phyllis had actually been conditioned to stay up late because there was a payoff or reward for doing this—relaxation, time to herself and a sugar ''high'' from all the sweets she consumed during this time.

We successfully broke this pattern by instructing Phyllis to do the following:

- Go to bed between 11:00 p.m. and midnight each evening. If you are unable to sleep after 15 minutes, get out of bed, go to another room and read or write letters. After 20 minutes, go back to bed and try again. By staying in bed tossing and turning, she would have been associating the bed with restlessness rather than sleep. After about seven nights of getting in and out of bed several times, she finally started falling asleep at a reasonable hour.
- Remove all sweets from the house. (While Bob liked an occasional dessert, he agreed to eat them only at lunch or when they went to a restaurant for dinner.)
- Stay out of the kitchen after 10:15 p.m. (after your stamina snack of fruit).
- Schedule a time just for *you* at some other time during the day. While her morning exercise program provided solitary time for her, she also spent ½ hour each evening listening to jazz music, one of her favorite pasttimes. She didn't want to take too much time out of the evening, since it was the only time that she and Bob were together alone.

Problem 4—Inadequate Stress Management at Work

Plan of Action:

Phyllis was obviously overworked in her job because of inadequate assistance. Also, the male assistant who resented her authority was causing her undue stress. She resented the fact that the men at her level in the company had larger staffs than she did.

I encouraged her to use my six-step remedy for executive stress (see Chapter 15) to manage her stress problems more effectively. In addition, we discussed the need for her to develop the stamina attitude, to believe that it was her responsibility to take charge of her stress problems and to do something about them.

After analyzing her work stress as my program suggests, Phyllis came to the following conclusions:

- Trying to "prove" her abilities by doing more than her male counterparts with less help was nonsense. All it proved was that her value to her company was being overlooked and that she was being placed in an inferior position.
- She had tried several ways to deal with the chauvinism and insecurity of her male assistant, all to no avail. She finally realized that this was not *her* problem, it was his. She was not going to put up with it anymore.
- Her stress was, at least in part, her own fault since she was the one who never complained about her plight at work.

On the strength of this analysis, Phyllis took several actions at work. First, she called her male assistant into her office and in a very matter-of-fact manner described how his difficulty in dealing with a woman's authority over him was a source of frustration for her and how it was negatively affecting the work that had to be done. Since she felt she had given him ample opportunity to change in the past, she then terminated his employment.

She next went to her employer, outlining her need for at least two more full-time assistants (plus one more to replace the man she had just fired). While she was at it, she reviewed her accomplishments since she had started with the company and asked for a raise in salary. At first her employer hesitated, but as soon as he realized how serious she was, he gave in to her requests. If he had not, she had been prepared to give her notice and send out her résumé. She had been so busy with her day-to-day life that she had failed to realize just how competent she was in her job.

Phyllis was especially pleased at how she dealt with both of these stressful encounters. She was direct and business-like. This approach to resolving her work stress gave her a tremendous boost of both relief and confidence.

Problem 5—Too Much to Do in Too Little Time

Plan of Action:

Actually, this problem resolved itself after each of the other problems were overcome. With her larger staff at work, she was able to delegate more work to others, giving her more time. Her husband took charge at home in the morning, allowing time for her exercise. With her newly adjusted income, she was able to pay the babysitter to stay a little later three evenings a week to prepare dinner. This allowed her to relax and spend uninterrupted time with her children when she arrived home from work.

Taking Better Care of Yourself

As a woman in the corporate world, you can benefit from the Hilton Head Executive Stamina Program just as Phyllis did. I find that many executive women put so much effort into their lives, trying to be all things to all people, that very little energy is left. You must realize that even though you can increase your endurance, there is a limit to anybody's energy.

As a woman manager, you have different and often more challenging stresses than men. You may even be breaking new ground in a career position that has, in the past, been a male domain. You must learn to deal with the stress that such a situation engenders. You may, at times, have to be more assertive and stick up for your rights with very little support from your colleagues. You may at other times have to be tolerant, and although not completely giving in, refrain from giving full vent to your true feelings.

The Hilton Head Executive Stamina Program can help you achieve more in less time, stay healthy in the process, reach levels of stamina and energy that you may not have thought possible and cope with the unique stresses that you encounter as a woman executive in the corporate world. Your new-found stamina will turn those seemingly insurmountable stresses into challenges with positive solutions.

17

▼

A Final Word

Now that I have outlined the entire stamina program, let me urge you to get started with these changes in your life. It is very easy to procrastinate, especially when it comes to changing your eating, exercising and thinking habits. What's that you're saying? You're too busy? This isn't the right time for you to make these changes? Well, there isn't any "right" time other than now, today, this instant!

We all tend to put things off and resist change. Our minds and bodies prefer the status quo, even if the status quo is one of fatigue, high blood pressure and stress. Sometimes you just have to *make* yourself change. Believe me, the rewards of this program are great. The executives who live the stamina lifestyle feel better than they have in years. They definitely do not feel deprived. They enjoy life more than ever. And their reserves of stamina allow them to live life to its fullest. They can throw themselves into the hectic corporate world, gathering more and more energy as they go.

A better, more productive life as an executive awaits you: a life in which your new-found stamina lets you be a better manager, capable of going strong long after others have faded. In addition, I continually hear reports from Hilton Head Health Institute graduates of improved concentration, memory and creativity. They are moving rapidly ahead in the corporate world, gaining advances in position, power and salary.

This program will allow you to become a *total executive:* one who has a well-rounded business, family and social life. You will be productive and perhaps even driven (but in a positive sense) because you will be the one in the driver's seat, in command of your own life. You will be the one responsible for a healthier, more energetic and longer life. As the years go on, you will be getting stronger and happier as you work and play at the height of your capabilities.

Just remember to put all five elements of the Hilton Head Executive Stamina Program into effect:

- The super stamina nutrition plan
- The stamina fitness plan
- The 20-minute resting-in-motion routine
- The three-minute mini-refresher
- The stamina attitude/stress management plan

As you put the program to use, check your progress at the end of each week to see how you are doing. Go over the past seven days and evaluate your performance on each of my five elements. Make sure you are not leaving anything out other than on an occasional basis. Then check your schedule the next week to see that you'll be able to follow the program. If you are going on a business trip, reread Chapter 13 on traveling to make certain you know exactly what to do.

The secret to success is *planning* and *consistency*. The more you follow this program, the more it will become second nature to you. You will be one of the successful graduates of the Hilton Head Executive Stamina Program who have become *super stamina executives*. Your life, like thousands of those before you, will have been changed forever!

Index